Architect's Guide to Arbitration
The Arbitration Act 1996

Architect's Guide to

Arbitration

The Arbitration Act 1996

Sarah Lupton

RIBA Publications

Published by RIBA Publications, a division of RIBA Companies Ltd, Finsbury Mission, 39 Moreland Street, London EC1V 8BB

ISBN 1 85946 030 5

Editor: Alaine Hamilton
Design and typography by RIBA Publications Design

Printed and bound by Biddles Ltd, Guildford

Contents

Foreword

By his Honour Judge Humphrey LLoyd QC
An Official Referee of the High Court of Justice

Arbitration is the construction industry's preferred method of resolving those disputes which survive despite all attempts to dispose of them by negotiation or by the decision of some wise person. The Arbitration Act 1996 is therefore important to anybody who works in or for the construction industry. primarily because for the first time an Act sets out in plain English the basic framework of arbitration as it is understood in England, Wales and Northern Ireland. (Scotland is both ahead, since it reformed its law some years ago, and behind, since it intends to make further changes.) But even such a well drafted Act requires explanation and illustration.

The role of an architect in expressing views and opinions in the form of certificates and other determinations or decisions has been traditionally and rightly described as 'the preventer of disputes'. In general it works well; if it did not the classic standard forms would have been changed long ago. The architect has a similar role in resolving differences and disputes, but where the certificate or decision may not please somebody the architect has to keep a weather eye open for what may happen next. Who is there better to guide an architect through that stage and the ensuing stages than another practising architect? However Sarah Lupton combines practice with a perceptive and analytical eye for the effect of law on architectural practice. She has been awarded a postgraduate degree in law (with merit). She has studied and has informed herself about arbitration and is now a Fellow of the Chartered Institute of Arbitrators. She lectures in and directs university courses on architectural practice and management. She has investigated and reported to the Joint Contracts Tribunal on performance specifications whose concepts require a very detailed knowledge of technical and legal issues. These are only some of her more recent activities. I have little doubt that this book will be an invaluable vade-mecum for every architect (and surveyor and engineer) who is likely to come into contact with the process of arbitration, particularly perhaps if the project (or dispute) is not of great value, for it is in this area that some of the bitterest battles can be fought.

Contact with arbitration may begin when architects are asked for advice on what form of dispute resolution might be selected. The Arbitration Act 1996 sets out in sections 1 and 33 (in particular) what is expected of arbitration. If arbitration is chosen, the agreement must be written. Sections 5 and 6 of the Act specify what will be sufficient for this purpose. However arbitration is largely what the parties make of it, so whilst the Act sets out what might be termed the 'default' positions on the powers of the arbitrator it also makes it clear that the parties are free to deviate from them. Sarah Lupton rightly points out that normally variances will form part of the original arbitration agreement or in the procedural rules published by well-known bodies, such as the JCT. However architects may be asked their views on other proposals or may have some of their own (eg on the vexed question of multi-party arbitration: see paragraph 7.36 onwards). They need to know that section 5(1) requires every agreement to be in writing and that what might be agreed in a meeting or conversation has also to meet the requirements of the Act.

Architects may also be involved in disputes during the course of the contract. Sarah Lupton notes the potential statutory adjudication schemes in paragraph 1.17. We have yet to see how they will work since that part of the Housing Grants, Construction and Regeneration Act 1996 is not yet effective. We do know that section 34 of the Arbitration Act 1996 now sets out the wide ambit of arbitrator's powers. Since arbitrators now have a statutory duty to avoid unnecessary delay and expense they are likely to be looking for the best way to establish the salient facts. Architects are in future likely to be both detached, as someone else may be concerned with sorting out disputes (eg an adjudicator) and less detached, because someone else may be sitting in judgment on them, unless the contract is administered punctiliously. So my forecast is that architects will have to be more concerned with ensuring that there are accurate records. Furthermore time spent in preparing agreed minutes or protocols of all stages of the work may avert disputes, for the possibility of later argument about events will be reduced. Study of section 7 of this book will help architects to understand what is needed if a dispute reaches an arbitration hearing. Experience shows that if the facts cannot be disputed because there were clear contemporary records then much else will fall into place. The procedures in the Act (like those of adjudication schemes) are likely to place a premium on the traditional independence of the architect. If the architect can demonstrate integrity (consistent with client relationship – see paragraph 6.24 in the section on discovery) the adjudicator and arbitrator may not have to decide to whom they should first turn for reliable account of what took place.

If an arbitration does happen then an architect may be called in to help the client or someone else. This guide contains a mass of practical points, eg the use of a typical Scott Schedule and case notes. Both at the time and certainly in retrospect, most disputes can be seen to be avoidable and unnecessary. I am sure that if the points to be found in this book are heeded some disputes should not get as far as arbitration or should be settled during its course.

Finally architects may become arbitrators and this work will undoubtedly help them in that task. Most of the Act does not contain innovations but is an exposition of what might be called 'best practice'. I have only touched on some of them. To have such a summary is a great practical advantage and to have both it and a straightforward and practical guide within the covers of one work is a double advantage.

Preface

The Arbitration Act 1996 received the Royal Assent on 17 June 1996, and apart from Sections 85–87, came into force on 31 January 1997. It now covers all arbitrations commenced after 31 January, where the seat of the arbitration is in England and Wales or Northern Ireland, even though the contract was entered into earlier and expressly refers to earlier legislation. The Act consolidates previous legislation, and puts much existing case law and accepted practice on a statutory footing.

The new Act has been greeted with enthusiasm and interest. It is written in clear and simple language and is generally 'user friendly'. The Act emphasises the flexibility and autonomy of arbitration by allowing the parties to tailor their arbitration to suit their own needs. It places a duty on the arbitrator, whilst ensuring that the parties are treated fairly, to conduct the arbitration in a way which avoids unnecessary delay and expense, and in a manner which suits the parties and the nature of the dispute. To assist in this the powers of the arbitrator are significantly increased from the position prior to the Act.

This Guide is intended for architects and other professionals involved in construction. Architects may become involved in arbitration in several ways. They may wish to advise their clients about dispute resolution methods at an early stage in a project, so that provision for appropriate methods is included in all contracts. Architects may also become directly involved in arbitration when disputes arise with their clients or between employer and contractor on construction contracts which they are administrating. Finally, architects may decide to train as arbitrators themselves. In all these situations a detailed understanding of the new Act and the potential it offers for effective forms of arbitration is essential.

This Guide gives a general overview of arbitration and discusses its legal framework, including the new Act, and the provisions included in construction contracts. It goes through the process of arbitration step by step outlining the duties and roles of the participants at each stage, including the appointment and obligations of the arbitrator, and the role of the courts in supporting the process. It describes the various forms the hearing and the award might take, and the methods by which objections or challenges can be made to the arbitration and the award.

The Guide assumes that the tribunal will be a sole arbitrator, as this is the usual practice in construction, rather than three arbitrators as is more common in shipping disputes. It deals only with domestic arbitration, and does not discuss international arbitration. The Guide assumes no prior knowledge of arbitration on the part of the reader, and though a basic understanding of the law is a great help in understanding the subject, it is not essential for reading the Guide. The full text of the published Act, with the exception of the Schedules, is included as Appendix A. A summary of all court cases cited is contained in Appendix B. Detailed references to arbitration law prior to the Act are kept to a minimum, so those looking for a comparative analysis should consult one of the more detailed legal commentaries. However, as architects may be involved with those who have extensive experience with arbitration before the Act, some of the more significant changes are pointed out so that architects may be alert to their implications.

The author is grateful to a number of people for their help in writing this Guide. In particular, she would like to thank Manos Stellakis, John Timpson and Stanley Cox for helpful comments on drafts of the text, and His Honour Judge Humphrey LLoyd QC for his comments on particular sections, and for kindly agreeing to write the foreword.

Glossary

Counsel
A barrister or a collective term for barristers.

Fit for Counsel
A phrase used to indicate that the arbitrator considers that the cost of engaging counsel was justified in regard to the Order on which the phrase is used.

Further and better particulars
Further information with respect to or clarification of a statement of claim, defence or counterclaim.

Hearsay
A statement, whether oral or documentary, made otherwise than by a witness giving oral evidence in the proceedings and which is tendered as evidence of the truth of the matters stated. For example, if an architect, when giving evidence, states that foundations were poured on a particular date, and he knows this because his Clerk of Works reported this at a particular meeting, this could be considered hearsay evidence with respect to establishing when the foundations were poured. However it is not hearsay with respect to proving that the workman made that statement. The Civil Evidence Act 1995 has abolished entirely the rule against hearsay evidence, stating that evidence cannot be excluded merely on the grounds that it is hearsay, though the Act contains some procedural safeguards.

Lien
A right to retain possession of another's property pending discharge of a debt.

Peremptory order
This repeats the original order, specifying a time for compliance and setting out the consequences for failure to comply.

Rules of the Supreme Court (RSC)
The rules formulated by the Supreme Court Rule Committee, which govern and regulate the practice and procedure in the Supreme Court of Judicature.

RSC Order 14: Summary judgment

Summary judgment is available where a plaintiff has lodged a claim, and the defendant has given notice of his intention to defend the action but the plaintiff can show that there is no defence to the claim. Its purpose is to enable the plaintiff to obtain a quick judgment where there is clearly no defence, or the defence is a point of law that can be shown very briefly to be unsustainable.

Scott v Avery

A type of arbitration clause named after *Alexander Scott v George Avery* (1856) 10 ER 1121 which establishes that the parties may make an arbitrator's award a condition precedent to the right to bring an action in court.

Scott Schedule

Named after the Official Referee, George Alexander Scott, this is also known as 'Official Referee's Schedule'. The Scott Schedule is used to summarise a claim which comprises a large number of separate items. It does not have a fixed format but is often presented in tabular form, typically comprising six to twelve columns which may include: the item number, brief details of the item, the amount being claimed, the respondent's estimate of the amount, the respondent's answer or comments and a column left for the arbitrator's own use.

Seat of the Arbitration

The place where the arbitration takes place. Determining the seat of an arbitration in the absence of agreement can be a complex legal question. It is quite possible, for example, for some of the meetings, or even the hearing, to take place in another country and for the seat to remain in the UK (*Mustill and Boyd 1989, p65*). Generally, however, any arbitration where all the meetings and the hearing are held in the UK, and where both parties are normally resident in the UK or are companies registered in the UK, is likely to fall under the Act.

Security for costs

The guarantee provided by the claimant in an arbitration reference to meet the costs if he fails in his claim.

Specific performance

A discretionary order given by the court to direct a person to perform his or her obligation under a contract. It is usually only used in situations where monetary compensation would be inadequate, for example where a party is ordered to return a unique painting. It is rarely used in construction, and an arbitrator is unlikely to award specific performance, due to the practical difficulties of specifying what is to be done, and in arranging supervision of the work.

Substantive law

The law governing the merits of the dispute, as opposed to the procedural law.

1 The nature of arbitration

1.01 Arbitration is a consensual process whereby two or more parties bring a dispute before a tribunal which makes a final and binding decision with respect to all matters raised. In construction, the tribunal is usually a single arbitrator. The arbitrator must decide the dispute impartially and treat both parties fairly during the arbitration, giving each a reasonable opportunity to present its case. The process is supported by the Arbitration Act 1996 (the Act), which sets out the powers and duties of the arbitrator, the rights and obligations of the parties, and the powers of the court available to support the process.

1.02 A dispute may come before an arbitrator in one of two ways. Either the parties may decide, after a dispute has arisen, that arbitration is their preferred method of resolving the dispute or, perhaps more likely, they may have agreed in advance under the terms of a contract that any dispute arising from that contract will be resolved through arbitration.

1.03 The parties may appoint an arbitrator themselves, once a dispute has arisen, or they may ask a professional institution to appoint one for them. Frequently an arbitration agreement will provide for a default mechanism whereby if the parties fail to agree on an arbitrator within a specified period of time either party may apply to a named institution to appoint one on its behalf.

1.04 The Act does not require an arbitrator to have any formal qualifications unless the parties have agreed that he or she should, and architects with no formal training in arbitration are sometimes appointed to act as arbitrator. However the arbitrator's role is a difficult one requiring a high degree of knowledge and skill, and parties increasingly demand evidence of experience, formal training and legal knowledge. The appointing institutions, including the RIBA, will generally only appoint arbitrators from panels of trained and experienced professionals who have demonstrated their competence under a formal method of assessment.

1.05 Once the arbitrator is appointed, he or she will normally guide the parties as to a suitable form of proceeding, so that mutually satisfactory arrangements can be made. If the parties cannot agree these matters, the Act gives the arbitrator the power to direct the form the proceedings take. A very wide variety of forms of arbitration are acceptable under the new Act, and Chapters 6 and 7 look at these in detail.

1.06   At the conclusion of the arbitration the arbitrator publishes his or her decision in the form of an award. This will set out the arbitrator's conclusions on all questions raised, and the reasons for reaching those conclusions. The award is binding and enforceable through a court of law. It is possible to challenge the award of an arbitrator, or to bring an appeal on a point of law, but the circumstances under which either can be done are very limited (*see Chapter 8*).

Comparison with other forms of dispute resolution

1.07   In deciding whether to use arbitration to resolve their disputes, the parties will be assessing it in relation to the available alternatives. These are to bring a claim through the courts, or to pursue another form of 'alternative dispute resolution' (ADR) such as mediation or adjudication. Their decision will depend on the nature of the dispute and the parties' circumstances in each case, and the following discussion points out some of the key differences and criteria which might influence their choice.

Arbitration compared with litigation

1.08   Litigation, unlike arbitration, does not require the consensus of the parties. It is the right of any citizen to bring an action in the courts for a breach of contract or a tortious wrong, therefore if one of the parties refuses to agree to arbitrate, litigation may be the only option.

1.09   Litigation cases which involve claims for amounts greater than £50,000 are normally heard in the High Court, and construction cases are usually heard in the Official Referees' Courts, a specialist department of the High Court which deals with technical or scientific cases. Procedures in court follow the Rules of the Supreme Court, with the timetable and other detailed arrangements being determined by the court. The case will be heard by a judge, and if it is heard in the High Court the parties must be represented by a barrister.

1.10   In arbitration, as the process is consensual, the parties are free to agree themselves on timing, place, representation and the individual arbitrator. This autonomy carries with it the benefits of increased convenience, and possibly savings in time and expense. The parties will be able to avoid the long waiting lists currently running at the High Court. In theory, at least, an arbitrator can be appointed immediately and the proceedings can be programmed to suit the parties. For parties located outside London, travelling to and accommodation near the Official Referees' Courts can be very expensive, therefore the ability to select a location will bring a considerable saving in costs. However in arbitration the parties will have to pay for the arbitrator and for renting the premises in which the arbitration is held, whereas in litigation the judge and the courtroom are free.

1.11   In arbitration the parties can select an arbitrator who has a technical background in the subject under dispute. Judges of the County Courts and High Court hear a wide variety of cases and will not generally have the technical knowledge of an arbitrator, with the exception of the Official Referees, who have extensive experience of technical construction disputes. The high standard achieved in these courts is one reached in practice by only a few arbitrators.

1.12   The legal knowledge of an arbitrator can never equal that of a judge, but there are several ways of compensating for this. The parties could select an arbitrator from the legal profession, if the matter in dispute is essentially one of law. If the arbitrator has a technical rather than a legal background, they could agree to the arbitrator taking legal advice, something the Act allows. The Act also gives the parties to an arbitration the right to raise a particular question of law in court (*see 7.19*).

1.13   The arbitrator has a wide variety of powers which can direct the parties to do or refrain from doing certain things during the course of the proceedings. However the court, which also has the majority of these powers, has more powerful sanctions at its disposal for noncompliance. It also has some powers which are not available to the arbitrator. For example, where a dispute between employer and main contractor is closely related to a dispute between main contractor and subcontractor, there may be many advantages in hearing both disputes together. The court has the power to direct this with respect to actions brought in court, whereas the arbitrator has no power to join related arbitrations unless all three parties agree. This is a significant disadvantage of arbitration, as construction disputes frequently involve many parties. Though joinder of actions can make the dispute more expensive for one or more of the parties, it is nevertheless unsatisfactory to have several arbitrators making decisions about the same or similar issues, and possibly reaching different conclusions. (*See the discussion in 7.36.*)

1.14   In court, the proceedings are open to the public and the press, and the judgment is published and widely available. In arbitration, the proceedings and the result can be kept private, something which is frequently of paramount importance in construction, and is often a deciding factor in selecting arbitration.

Arbitration compared with other forms of ADR

1.15   Arbitration can be contrasted with other forms of ADR, such as mediation or conciliation, in that the latter two have no supporting legislation, at least with respect to construction disputes. The terms 'mediation' and 'conciliation' have no fixed definitions in practice. The procedures in these alternative methods may vary considerably but are usually a voluntary consensual process involving a third party who assists the disputants in reaching a mutually acceptable resolution of their dispute. As mediation and conciliation have no formal sanctions to deal with recalcitrant parties, they depend throughout on mutual cooperation, and the proceedings can break down.

1.16   The final decision is usually in the form of a mutually agreed set of terms, and the process therefore avoids the adversarial atmosphere which pervades any form of dispute resolution where a third party has the right to impose a decision on the parties. Encouraging the parties to reach an agreement rather than simply determining who is right builds up mutual understanding, and is particularly useful where parties wish to preserve a long term business relationship. The agreement reached is frequently embodied in a contract that the parties sign. If either of the parties subsequently breaches this contract, the other can bring an action in court, but the contract is not directly enforceable in the way that an arbitrator's award would be. There are also some hybrid procedures, for example the ICE Conciliation Procedure, where if the parties fail to reach agreement the conciliator prepares a Recommendation, which the parties agree in advance they will honour.

1.17   The term 'adjudication' deserves a special note. Following the implementation of the relevant sections of the Housing Grants, Construction and Regeneration Act 1996 (HGCRA), any party to a construction contract will have the right to refer any dispute arising under the contract to a process of 'adjudication' which must comply with criteria detailed in that Act under Section 108.

1.18   In the case of *Cape Durasteel Ltd v Rosser and Russell Building Services Ltd*, 1995 Judge LLoyd said (at p85): 'It is plain that "adjudication" taken by itself means a process by which a dispute is resolved in a judicial manner. It is equally clear that "adjudication" has yet no special meaning in the construction industry (which is not surprising since it is a creature of contract and contractual procedures utilising an "adjudicator" vary as do forms of contract).' Due to the particular circumstances in that case, which predated the HGCRA, and the parties' intentions regarding the nature of the process, in particular its finality, the reference to 'adjudication' was construed as arbitration, with the result that the parties could rely on the statutory backing to arbitration. Following the implementation of the HGCRA, a reference to 'adjudication' in any contract governed by that legislation is likely to be treated as a reference to statutory adjudication. In any case, even if the parties intended something entirely different by what they describe as 'adjudication', each party would still have the right to adjudication as provided for by the HGCRA.

1.19   Adjudication under the HGCRA will resemble litigation in that, being a statutory right, it is not consensual. Of course this right does not have to be exercised, and if both parties wish to resolve their dispute in some other way they may do so. The HGCRA gives only minimal requirements for the form adjudication should take: the referral to an adjudicator must take place within seven days of the notice to adjudicate; the adjudicator must reach a decision within 28 days; he or she must decide the matter impartially, and the decision is binding until finally determined by arbitration or litigation, or until agreed by the parties. It is intended as a 'quick fix' solution to construction disputes, and in particular to avoid the problem of subcontractors having payments withheld from them which they are unable to claim except through what are seen as the lengthy and expensive processes of arbitration or litigation.

1.20   However, as the timescales are very short, if the dispute involves anything of complexity it is possible that one of the parties will be unhappy with the decision and it will be raised again in a further tribunal. The challenge could come about in two ways: either the original question could be raised again or, where the dissatisfied party has not honoured the adjudicator's decision, a claim could be brought for breach of this obligation. The tribunal will be arbitration if the contract contains an arbitration agreement which covers this dispute (*see 4.15*). It is quite likely, therefore, that once the HGCRA is implemented many arbitrations will be following in the wake of an adjudicator's decision.

1.21 It is important to note that any further proceedings would not normally be an appeal from the adjudicator's decision in the way that an appeal may be brought in court, in certain circumstances, from an arbitrator's award. In other words the arbitrator would not be considering whether the adjudicator had reached the right answer given the evidence which was available to the adjudicator at that time. The arbitrator would be considering the question again from scratch, and would therefore hear all the evidence, including new evidence, which the parties bring forward in the arbitration (*see 7.15*). The only exception to this would be if the parties had agreed some restriction on the ability of a further tribunal to review the adjudicator's decision, for example if they had agreed in advance that certain decisions of the adjudicator would be final.

2   The legal framework

2.01   The legal framework for arbitration is to be found in the Act and in relevant case law. The Act is a comprehensive piece of legislation covering, amongst other things, the powers and duties of the arbitrator, the rights and obligations of the parties, and the powers of the court in relation to arbitration. This Chapter describes the structure and scope of the Act. Detailed analysis of specific provisions of the Act will be made in the remaining Chapters of the Guide.

2.02   The Act allows for many of its provisions to be altered or supplemented by agreement of the parties. This may be done in either the parties' original agreement to submit the dispute to arbitration (*see Chapter 3*), or in supplementary agreements made as the arbitration progresses. Reference must therefore be made to these agreements as well as to the Act in order to determine the powers and duties of the parties, the arbitrator and the courts in any particular arbitration.

2.03   At the time of writing there is no reported case law relating specifically to the Act. Much of the existing case law concerning arbitration has been either incorporated into or superseded by the Act. Some case law does, however, give guidance as to the possible interpretation of the Act: in particular how the arbitrator's discretion should be exercised. It also throws light on some questions which the Act does not cover. These issues will be considered in the relevant sections of the Guide.

Introduction to the Arbitration Act 1996

2.04   The Act received the Royal Assent on 17 June 1996 and, apart from Sections 85–87, came into force on 31 January 1997. It repeals Part I of the Arbitration Act 1950, the Arbitration Acts of 1975 and 1979, and the Consumer Agreement Act 1988. In other words, it replaces all previous legislation regarding arbitration, except for certain parts of the 1950 Act which are concerned with the enforcement of foreign awards.

2.05   It extends to England and Wales and Northern Ireland and governs an arbitration where the seat is in England and Wales or Northern Ireland (S.2(1)). The term 'seat' means the place where the arbitration takes place (*see Glossary*). Section 3 of the Act defines the seat of the arbitration as being 'the judicial seat of the arbitration' designated either by the parties, or any institution, person or the arbitrator, providing the parties have awarded them this power. If the parties cannot agree on the seat, and in the unlikely event that they refuse to invest either an institution or the arbitrator with the right to decide, then this would be a question of law which could be referred to a court. To avoid any dispute it is good practice to specify the seat in the arbitration agreement.

2.06   The Act applies to all arbitrations commenced on or after 31 January 1997 regardless of when the arbitration agreement was entered into. The statutory instrument which brought the Act into force, the Arbitration Act 1996 (Commencement No 1) Order 1996 (SI 1996 No 3146 (C96)), sets out transitional provisions whereby the old law continues to apply to arbitrations commenced before 31 January 1997. The transitional provisions also provide that Section 46(1)(b), which allows the parties to agree that the arbitrator may decide the dispute in accordance with considerations other than the law (*see* *8.01*), will not apply unless the arbitration agreement was entered into after 31 January 1997.

2.07   Generally speaking the Act has been greeted with much praise and enthusiasm. It is comprehensive, clearly set out and avoids using technical terms, all of which make it accessible to the non-lawyer. It clarifies the law in relation to arbitration by consolidating previous legislation and absorbing points of law which were previously distributed amongst a mass of case law.

2.08   The Act provides the arbitrator with a wide range of powers, not all of which were previously available. It also reforms the powers available to the courts to supervise arbitral proceedings and entertain challenges to awards, in some respects limiting them compared with the pre-Act position. One of the intentions of the new Act was to make the UK a more attractive centre for international arbitration:

'It represents, given the current external pressures and opinion from the world of arbitration outside England, a careful piece of diplomacy designed to attract international arbitration to England by simultaneously offering greatly increased powers and discretions to arbitrators accompanied by apparently tightly restricted powers of review or of appeal from arbitrators, though still preserving the occasional right of the courts in the last resort to deal with any serious cases of excesses of jurisdiction which can be seen to disregard the consent of the parties, or with the most serious lapses by arbitrators in conducting arbitrations or in framing their awards.'
(*Wallace 1997a, p93*)

2.09   The article from which this quotation is taken expresses concern over the wide range of issues which are subject to the parties' agreement, which could leave many traps for inexperienced parties and arbitrators, and emphasises the need for careful drafting of agreements to arbitrate and procedural rules to fill in the gaps. If these dangers can be successfully overcome the Act undoubtedly opens the door to more flexible and efficient arbitration.

2.10   In addition to the Act, an entirely new Rule of the Supreme Court, RSC Order 73, came into force on the same day. It sets out the procedure for making applications to the court connected with arbitration, termed under the Order 'arbitration applications', including applications to stay judicial proceedings, to determine issues as to jurisdiction, to enforce peremptory orders, to secure the attendance of witnesses, to provide security for costs, to challenge the award on grounds of jurisdiction or serious irregularity and for leave to appeal on a question of law arising out of the award. All these are discussed under the relevant Chapters of the Guide.

The structure and scope of the Act

2.11   Section 1, unusually for a piece of legislation, sets out the general principles behind the Act which can be summarised as follows:
   · fair resolution by an impartial tribunal;
   · no unnecessary delay or expense;
   · freedom of the parties to decide procedures;
   · some safeguards to protect the public interest.

2.12   These general principles may be used as a guide in interpreting the rest of the Act, and would be used by a court when it is required to construe the Act, for example in resolving any areas of ambiguity.

2.13   Generally the Sections of the Act are of two types: those that apply to any arbitration falling under the Act, and which cannot be excluded by agreement, and those that act as default provisions, coming into place only when the parties have made no agreement to the contrary. Provisions that always apply are listed in Schedule 1 and are summarised in Table 1 below. Those provisions which the Act expressly makes 'subject to the agreement of the parties' are summarised in Table 2. The remaining sections of Part I of the Act concern its application and definitions used, and generally speaking

Table 1. Mandatory provisions of the Act (from Schedule 1)

Section	Subject
9–11	Stay of legal proceedings
12	Power of court to extend agreed time limits
13	Application of the Limitation Acts
24	Power of court to remove arbitrator
26(i)	Effect of death of arbitrator
28	Liability of parties for fees and expenses of arbitrator
29	Immunity of arbitrator
31	Objection to substantive jurisdiction of arbitrator
32	Determination of preliminary point of jurisdiction
33	General duty of arbitrator
37(2)	Items to be treated as expenses of arbitrator
40	General duties of the parties
43	Securing the attendance of witnesses
56	Power to withhold award in cases of non payment
60	Effectiveness of agreement for payment of costs in any event
66	Enforcement of award
67–68	Challenging the award: substantive jurisdiction and serious irregularity and
70–71	Supplementary provisions, effect of order of court so far as relating to those sections
72	Saving for rights of persons who take no part in proceedings
73	Loss of right to object
74	Immunity of arbitral institution etc
75	Charge to secure payment of solicitors costs

these cannot be affected by contrary agreement of the parties (*Harris, Planterose et al. 1996*).

Implications for standard forms of appointment, Joint Contracts Tribunal (JCT) contracts and arbitration rules

2.14   At the time of writing, neither the JCT standard forms of contract nor the JCT Arbitration Rules have been revised to take on board the new Act, although amendments are expected in the near future. The JCT have published a 'Note to Users' regarding the transitional position (*JCT 1997*). Any document making reference to the old legislation should be amended to refer to the new Act, and the Note sets out how this should be done with respect to the JCT Standard Forms.

2.15   A new set of arbitration rules, 'The Construction Industry Model Arbitration Rules' (CIMAR), has recently been published by the Society of Construction Arbitrators, which is suggesting that if CIMAR was adopted across the construction industry this would result in a uniform procedural basis for arbitration. The rules directly address the new Act, and may be adopted by the JCT in place of the JCT rules.

2.16   With regard to architects' appointment documents, the RIBA Architect's Services: Small Works refers expressly to the Arbitration Act 1996, and other standard forms will be updated.

2.17   An arbitration would not be invalidated because it arose from an arbitration agreement referring to the old legislation, as the new Act would automatically apply by operation of the Commencement Order (*see 2.06*). Where there is dispute as to how a matter in the agreement should be interpreted in the light of the new Act, the parties could refer the question to the arbitrator.

3 The agreement

3.01   An agreement to arbitrate can be made either after a dispute has
        arisen between the parties, often termed an 'ad hoc' submission, or in
        advance, as an 'agreement to refer' future disputes to arbitration. The
        latter is by far the most commonly found type in construction, and in
        the remainder of the Guide any reference to an arbitration agreement
        will mean an agreement embodied in another contract. Such
        agreements are to be found, for example, in all of the JCT standard
        forms of contract, and in the RIBA forms of appointment, as well as
        in many other standard forms of contract and appointment produced
        by other institutions. Notable exceptions are the second edition of the
        Engineering and Construction Contract, which does not contain a
        clear binding agreement to arbitrate (*see analysis of the arbitration
        clauses in Cornes, 1996*), and the proposed new NEC Short Contract
        which makes no reference to arbitration at all.

3.02   The advantage of an 'agreement to refer' is that once a dispute has
        arisen it may be very difficult for the parties to make an objective
        decision regarding an appropriate method for its resolution. Where a
        contract contains an arbitration agreement, this effectively ensures
        that the dispute will be resolved by arbitration, unless both parties
        later decide that they would prefer some other method. (*Note,
        however, the exceptions with respect to consumer agreements discussed
        under 3.18.*) If one party changes its mind and initiates legal
        proceedings, the courts will support the party who wishes to proceed
        with the arbitration. In fact the Act requires the court to place a
        temporary halt, termed a 'stay', on any court proceedings that have
        been commenced provided there is a valid agreement to arbitrate and
        certain conditions are fulfilled (*see 4.15*). The court also has the
        power to order a party to appoint an arbitrator, or to appoint an
        arbitrator itself, should the procedures agreed by the parties break
        down (*see 4.05 and 4.06*). To take advantage of these powers it is
        therefore advisable to include an 'agreement to refer' in any contract
        where arbitration is likely to be the preferred method of dispute
        resolution.

Requirements of the Act

3.03   Section 6 of the Act defines an arbitration agreement as follows:
        'In this Part an "arbitration agreement" means an agreement to
        submit to arbitration present or future disputes (whether they are
        contractual or not)' (S.6(1)).

The definition makes it clear that the arbitration agreement may relate to disputes that are non-contractual, for example tortious claims. The Section adds that reference in an agreement to a written arbitration clause will constitute an arbitration agreement (S.6(2)), as will reference to another document containing an arbitration clause. This resolves a problematic area of law whereby reference to a standard form containing an arbitration agreement, without referring specifically to the arbitration clause, had been held not to be a valid agreement to arbitrate (*Aughton Ltd v M F Kent Services Ltd*, 1991).

3.04 Section 5 states that the provisions of the Act only apply to agreements in writing, which include:
- agreements made in writing but unsigned (S.5(2)(a));
- agreements made by exchange of communications in writing (S.5(2)(b));
- agreements evidenced in writing (S.5(2)(c)), including agreements recorded by one party or by a third party, with the authority of the parties to the agreement (S.5(4));
- agreements other than in writing which refer to terms which are in writing (S.5(3));
- an exchange of written submissions in arbitral or legal proceedings in which the existence of an agreement otherwise than in writing is alleged and not denied (S.5(5)).

3.05 'In writing' includes being recorded by any means, which would include tape and electronic products. The definition under the Act is therefore very broad and, in particular, it covers an oral agreement to incorporate a standard form of agreement into a contract, or an exchange of letters, situations which frequently occur in construction. The requirement to be in writing covers all matters agreed, for example any agreement to adopt procedural rules or to preclude any of the default procedures in the Act, or any subsequent additional agreement.

3.06 Unless otherwise agreed by the parties, the agreement does not become invalid simply because an agreement in which it is incorporated is invalid, or did not come into existence, or has become ineffective (S.7). This is termed the 'separability' of the arbitration agreement. The provision is useful where, for example, there is doubt about the formation or continuing existence of a construction contract, and where one party wishes to raise these issues in arbitration, and therefore to rely on an arbitration agreement incorporated into that contract. Even if it is unclear as to whether agreement was reached on all the terms of the contract, the agreement may still survive provided that it can be shown that the parties had agreed on that part. The arbitration agreement itself would still have to exist within the terms defined above, and any question about its validity would need to be examined as a separate matter (*see 3.16*).

Issues to be addressed in the agreement

3.07　One of the underlying principles of the Act is the freedom it allows the parties to tailor their arbitration to suit their own needs. Though the Act allows the parties to agree matters at any time, if the parties use the arbitration agreement to set out the more detailed provisions which they would like to govern their arbitration, there will be less room for argument later. This can be done either within the agreement itself or more conveniently by reference to one of the many available sets of procedural rules which, provided the reference is clear, then become a binding part of the arbitration agreement (*see 6.02*).

3.08　For the sake of clarity, either the agreement or the rules should deal systematically with all the 'unless otherwise agreed by the parties' provisions in the Act (*see Table 2*), either confirming that the default provisions apply or setting out the parties' agreed alternative. Using these provisions as checklist will ensure that the parties address all the more important issues which are matters for their decision, and will leave the arbitrator in no doubt as to the parties' intentions. In particular the arbitration agreement should cover the following:
- procedural issues raised in Section 34 of the Act (*see Chapters 6 and 7*);
- powers of the arbitrator, in particular the power to order security for costs (*see 7.25*), to order provisional relief (*see 7.34*), to limit the recoverable costs of the arbitration (*see 8.18*), to award compound interest (*see 8.09*);
- powers of the courts, in particular the power to determine a preliminary point of law (*see 7.19*);
- the right of the parties to appeal on a point of law (*see 8.30*);
- provisions for multi-party arbitrations (*see 7.36*);
- the power to open up and review decisions and certificates of the architect (*see 5.13*).

Table 2. Provisions of the Act which are subject to the agreement of the parties

Section	Subject
7	Separability of arbitration agreement
8	Whether agreement discharged by death of a party
14	Commencement of arbitral proceedings
15–23, 25, 27	The arbitral tribunal: appointment, composition, revocation of authority, resignation of arbitrator
30	Competence of tribunal to rule on its own jurisdiction
34–36	Procedural and evidential matters, consolidation of proceedings, representation
37–39	Power of tribunal to appoint experts, legal advisors or assessors, to order a claimant to provide security for costs, to give directions in relation to property, to direct examination of witnesses, to make provisional awards
41	Powers of tribunal in case of party's default
42	Enforcement of peremptory orders of tribunal
44	Court's powers exercisable in support of arbitral proceedings
45	Determination of a preliminary point of law
46–55	The award: rules applicable, part awards, remedies, interest, extension of time for making, settlement, form, place where treated as made, date, notification
57–58	Correction of award, effect of award
63–65	Matters concerning costs
69	Appeal on point of law
76–79	Services of notices etc, reckoning of periods of time, power of court to extend time limits

Typical agreements, including standard form contract provisions

3.09   A typical 'agreement to refer' can be found in JCT 80. It is contained in article 5, clause 41, and the rules to which clause 41.9 refers. Article 5 sets out the basic commitment to resolve all disputes by arbitration:

'If any dispute or difference as to the construction of this Contract or any matter or thing of whatsoever nature arising thereunder or in connection therewith shall arise between the Employer or the Architect on his behalf and the Contractor either during the progress or after the completion or abandonment of the Works or after the determination of the employment of the Contractor, except under clause 31 [*statutory tax deduction scheme*] to the extent provided in clause 31.9 or under clause 3 of the VAT Agreement, it shall be and is hereby referred to arbitration in accordance with clause 41.'

3.10   The article is framed widely to catch the vast majority of disputes that would arise in the normal course of events. This includes matters such as the exact agreement reached between the parties. JCT 80 clause 41.1 outlines the procedure for commencing the arbitration as follows:

'When the Employer or the Contractor requires a dispute or difference . . . to be referred to arbitration then either the Employer or the Contractor shall give written notice to the other to such effect and such dispute or difference shall be referred to the arbitration and final decision of a person to be agreed between the parties as the Arbitrator, or, upon failure so to agree within 14 days after the date of the aforesaid written notice, of a person to be appointed as the Arbitrator on the request of either the Employer or the Contractor by the person named in the Appendix.'

3.11   JCT 80 clause 41.2 covers multi-party arbitrations, which are discussed under 7.35 below. Clause 41.3 requires that only certain types of dispute may be brought to arbitration before Practical Completion. These are:
·   disputes on articles 3 and 4 (the terms Architect and Quantity Surveyor);
·   whether the issue of an instruction is empowered by the contract;
·   whether a certificate has been improperly withheld or is not in accordance with the contract;
·   whether a determination under clause 22C4.3.1 (subsequent to loss or damage to the Works) will be just and equitable;
·   disputes under clauses 4.1 (Contractor's objection to an instruction), 8.4 (work not in accordance with the contract), 8.5 (work not being carried out in a proper and workmanlike manner), 18.1 (partial possession), 23.3.2 (Employer's use of the site to store goods), or clause 25 (extensions of time).

Clearly these are all matters that would be best decided during the course of the contract, as they all have immediate knock-on effects. All other disputes must be raised after Practical Completion.

3.12   Clause 41.4 sets out certain powers of the arbitrator, including the power to rectify the contract, and the power to open up and review decisions and certificates of the architect. The powers of the arbitrator are discussed under 5.13, but it should be noted that it is unlikely that the arbitrator would have the power to open up and review unless expressly given it in the agreement.

3.13   The remaining sub-clauses are as follows:
- 41.5 states that the award of the arbitrator shall be final and binding on the parties. This would be the default position under Section 58 of the Act (*see 8.26*);
- 41.6 covers appeals. It sets out what would be the default position under Sections 45 and 69 (*see 8.30*);
- 41.7 states that the law of England shall be the proper law of the contract. This defines the law applicable to the substance of the dispute (*see 8.01*);
- 41.8 covers re-appointment should the arbitrator die or cease to act, and therefore sets out the parties' own agreement with respect to Section 27 of the Act;
- 41.9 states that the arbitration shall be conducted in accordance with the JCT Arbitration Rules.

3.14   The above clauses will be amended in the light of the new Act. The JCT Arbitration Rules referred to in clause 41.9 are also being revised. The JCT's 'Note to Users' states that 'the existing Arbitration Rules are compatible with the provisions of the Arbitration Act 1996 and can continue to be used meantime'. It does, however, point out that some of the notes to the Rules are not an accurate statement of the law under the Act.

3.15   Rules typically cover procedural issues concerned with events following appointment of the arbitrator and up to and including the hearing. They set out specific steps that the arbitrator and the parties must take, and time frames in which they must be taken. They also confer additional powers on the arbitrator, many of which are now expressly conferred by the Act. Section 4 of the Act makes it clear that if any Rules conflict with the Act this would constitute an 'agreement otherwise'. The procedures outlined under the JCT Rules are discussed under Chapter 6.

Doubt over the existence of an agreement

3.16   An arbitrator will normally ask to see the parties' arbitration agreement at the earliest opportunity in order to confirm that he or she has authority to decide the matters raised by the parties. This authority is termed the arbitrator's 'jurisdiction'. Where there is any possibility of misunderstanding, or the agreement is in any way unclear but the parties wish to proceed with the arbitration, the arbitrator may ask that they evidence their agreement in writing.

3.17   If a party wishes to challenge the jurisdiction of the arbitrator by questioning whether there is a valid agreement to arbitrate it has two choices: it can ask the arbitrator to decide the matter, or it can ask the court. Section 30(1)(a) of the Act gives the arbitrator, unless otherwise agreed by the parties, the right to determine whether there is a valid arbitration agreement. There is clearly a tautology involved, and the question of whether an arbitrator could determine the existence of an agreement under which he or she had been appointed was much debated in the years preceding the Act. The Act clearly gives the arbitrator this power. However the Act also specifically states in Section 30(2) that the arbitrator's ruling may be challenged by appeal or review (*see 8.29*). This provision is mandatory and in effect prevents the possibility of a party being 'trapped' by the result of an arbitration which was invalid. The options and procedures for raising questions of jurisdiction are discussed in more detail in 5.24–26.

Consumer arbitration agreements

3.18   Though an arbitration agreement entered into in advance of a dispute arising would normally be binding on the parties to the agreement, it should be noted that there are now exceptions due to the combined operation of the Arbitration Act 1996 and the Unfair Terms in Consumer Contracts Regulations 1994. The Regulations apply to all contracts where one party is a consumer, by which is meant that the party is acting outside of the course of their business, and to all terms which have not been individually negotiated. These would include, for example, arbitration clauses in standard forms of contract. Under Section 91 of the Act arbitration agreements to which the Regulations apply are automatically non-binding where the amount in dispute falls within a certain limit. The limit is yet to be set, but is likely to be close to that set for small claims court based arbitration, which is currently £3,000. For larger claims the agreement will only be non-binding if the consumer can show that it is unfair, for example by showing that it creates a significant imbalance of power. This is unlikely to be the case, but as the legislation is recent it remains to be seen how it will be applied in practice. (*See discussion in Harris, Planterose et al, 1996, p304–10.*)

4   Commencing the arbitration

4.01   The Act leaves the parties free to agree on the procedure for appointment of an arbitrator (S.16). An arbitration is usually commenced by one party sending the other a notice requesting that the dispute that has arisen between them be referred to arbitration. This notice can take a wide variety of forms. Where an arbitrator has already been named in the agreement, the notice will simply indicate the particular dispute to be referred. Where an arbitrator is still to be appointed, a notice to concur in the appointment of an arbitrator will be served by one party on the other, usually offering a shortlist of three arbitrators who would be acceptable to the party serving the notice. JCT 80 article 5 requires simply that a written notice is sent. However, it is good practice to name the contract under which the dispute has arisen, the arbitration agreement under which the notice is being served, and to indicate in outline the subject matter of the dispute. A specimen notice is given as Figure 1.

4.02   Following receipt of the notice, if it concerns a dispute under a contract which an architect is administrating, the client may turn to the architect for advice. The architect could give general guidance at

Figure 1. Specimen notice to arbitrate

Dear Sirs

Ref. (project name)
Notice of arbitration

We give you notice that a dispute has arisen from our contract with you for the above project, due to the failure of the Architect to grant an extension of time as requested in our letter of .... We now require that this dispute be referred to arbitration in accordance with Article 5 and clause 41 of our contract.

We submit to you the names of three arbitrators and request that you agree to the appointment of one of them as the arbitrator in this reference.

If we do not receive a reply within 14 days of this notice, or if all the nominees are rejected without the substitution of a nominee acceptable to ourselves, we will apply to the President of the RIBA for the appointment of an arbitrator in accordance with clause 41.1 of the contract.

Yours ...

this point, but should avoid being drawn in to act as advocate for the client. Generally parties to an arbitration take legal advice, except in the simplest of disputes (*see 7.04*). If the notice concerns a contract between architect and client, the architect should inform his or her professional indemnity insurers of the situation. It may also be prudent for the architect to notify his or her insurers where the notice concerns a dispute under the main contract, depending on the nature of the dispute and the terms of the policy.

4.03   If the parties cannot agree on a particular arbitrator, then they may apply to an appointing institution to make an appointment on their behalf. They can agree to do this after the dispute arises, or they may have named an appointing institution in their agreement to arbitrate. All JCT forms allow for an appointing institution to be named in advance, and for either party to apply for an appointment should the parties fail to reach agreement on an arbitrator within 14 days of the notice to refer being served (*see 3.10*).

4.04   The RIBA, the Chartered Institute of Arbitrators, the ICE, and the RICS are some of the main institutions that currently act as appointing bodies. Forms are available from the RIBA for the use of parties applying to the President for the appointment of an arbitrator (*see Fig 2*). Most institutions will have a similar preferred procedure, but in the absence of any requirements the letter requesting an appointment should normally repeat all information given in the notice.

4.05   If the parties fail to appoint, unless otherwise agreed any party may apply to the court to appoint under Section 18 of the Act. Similarly, if any appointing authority fails to appoint, any party may apply to the court (S.19). The court would take into account any agreement the parties may have made regarding the qualifications of the arbitrator, and though they are not bound by that agreement, it is clear that they would normally follow it. As the court does not maintain a panel of arbitrators, it is a good idea for the party applying to put forward names of arbitrators in the application. The party should of course establish the willingness of the arbitrators to act before suggesting them.

Figure 2. RIBA application form

Royal Institute of British Architects, 66 Portland Place, London W1N 4AD

Appointment of an Arbitrator

Note: This form is to be used where the dispute arises under a building contract or other agreement wherein there is provision for arbitration. **A/B**

PART 1
this part only to be filled in by applicant

Regarding the agreement dated the _____ day of _____ and made

between _____ of the one part

and _____ of the other part and where there is an arbitration agreement.

WHEREAS a dispute or difference has arisen in connection therewith

I/We hereby ask the President of the Royal Institute of British Architects to appoint an arbitrator to hear and determine the matter.

As a Condition of the Appointment I/We jointly and severally agree as follows:
(1) To provide adequate security for the due payment of the fees and expenses of the Arbitrator if he so requires.
(2) To pay the fees and expenses of the Arbitrator whether the Arbitration reaches a Hearing or not.

(Signed)
_____

of _____
_____

(Signed)
_____

of _____
_____

Dated this _____ day of _____ 19_____

PART 2

I hereby appoint
_____

of _____
_____

Arbitrator in the above matter.

(Signed)
_____
President of the Royal Institute of British Architects
Dated this _____ day of _____ 19_____

I hereby accept the appointment in the above matter.

(Signed)
_____

1/97   Dated this _____ day of _____ 19_____

4.06   In addition to making the appointment itself (S.18(3)(d)), the court
        may exercise the following powers in relation to the appointment:
        ·   The power to give directions (S.18(3)(a))
            The court could use this, for example, to direct one of the parties to
            take steps necessary in the making of an appointment.
        ·   The power to direct the tribunal to be consisted by appointments
            already made (S.18(3)(b))
            This could be used where two arbitrators have failed to appoint an
            umpire, or where there are more than two parties but only two
            have made appointments.
        ·   The power to revoke appointments made (S.18(3)(c))
            This could be used to redress the balance where one party has
            appointed its own arbitrator but the other has had an arbitrator
            imposed by the court.

When does a 'dispute' arise?

4.07   Sometimes there can be doubt over what constitutes a 'dispute', and
        when it has come into existence. Generally speaking a dispute arises
        when a claim has been made by one party and rejected by the other,
        and that rejection has not been accepted (*Cruden Construction Ltd v
        Commission for the New Towns*, 1994; *Monmouthshire County Council
        v Costelloe & Kemple*, 1965). However in some circumstances the
        courts have found that a claim alone with no response from the other
        party may constitute a dispute. The contract can itself give a special
        meaning to the term 'dispute', for example in the 6th edition of the
        ICE main contract a dispute may not be referred to arbitration unless
        it has first been referred to the decision of the engineer. This would
        not be the case with JCT 80 where the term 'dispute' should be
        understood in its ordinary meaning.

Time limit on appointment

4.08   Where the arbitration agreement places a time limit on the right to
        refer the dispute to arbitration, by requiring that some step in
        commencing proceedings must be taken within a specified period of
        time, the court may by order extend the time (S.12(1)). It applies only
        to requirements that arbitration must be started within a specific
        time, which would normally be a shorter period than that set by
        statute (*see 4.10*). The court's powers do not extend to the relief
        from other contractual provisions, for example with respect to the

conclusiveness provisions relating to the Final Certificate in JCT 80 clause 30.9.3.

4.09   The party must give notice to the other party, and must have explored any available arbitral process for extending the time. The court will only make an order if it is satisfied either that particular circumstances have arisen which could not have been within the contemplation of the parties when they agreed to the time limit, or that the conduct of one of the parties would make it unjust to hold the other to that limit (S.12(3)). The power to extend the time bar also applies to any pre-arbitral dispute resolution processes which must be exhausted before arbitration begins, so the court would have this power with respect to any time bar agreed on adjudication (S.12(1)(b)). The power to extend cannot be exercised to extend periods set by the Limitation Acts (*see below*). If the court extends time it may set conditions with which the parties must comply.

The Limitation Acts

4.10   Limitation periods apply to claims brought in arbitration in the same way that they would apply to actions brought in court. In the case of claims for breach of contract, the claim must be brought within six years from the particular breach which is the subject of the claim, with the limitation period being twelve years if the contract is executed as a deed (Limitation Act 1980 S.5). In the case of a claim against a contractor for defective work it is generally thought that the period will run from the date of the Final Certificate, even though the particular work which is the subject of the claim was carried out earlier than that date. For claims in tort, the period is six years from the accrual of the cause of action (Limitation Act 1980 S.2). In the case of building defects this would be six years from when the damage occurred. The Latent Damage Act 1986 extends this for claims not involving personal injury to either six years from the accrual of the cause of action, or three years from the 'starting date', whichever is the later, subject to an overriding time limit of 15 years from the negligent act. The 'starting date' is the latest date when the claimant had both the knowledge required to bring an action for damages in respect of the relevant damage, and a right to bring the action. (For a detailed explanation see *Cornes*, 1994, Chapter 12.)

4.11   The Act expressly states that the Limitation Act 1980 applies to the proceedings (S.13). Unless the parties agree when the arbitration has

commenced for the purposes of the Limitation Act 1980, then Section 14 of the Act gives three possible dates for the commencement of the arbitration:
- in cases where the arbitrator is named in the agreement, at the date when one party sends a notice to the other requiring the matter to be referred to arbitration;
- in cases where the arbitrator is appointed by the parties, at the date of the notice requiring the appointment of an arbitrator (notice of the dispute itself may have been given earlier);
- in the case of appointment by a third party, at the date of notice to that third party requesting an appointment.

If the award or part of the award is set aside, the court can order that the period of time between the commencement of the arbitration and the setting aside of the award be excluded (S.13(2)).

4.12   The Act also states that the existence of a clause which provides that no action in a court of law can be started until an arbitration award has been made, frequently termed a '*Scott v Avery*' clause, will have no effect on the determination of the date at which the cause of action accrued for the purposes of calculating the limitation period for bringing a claim (S.13(3)).

Concluding the appointment

4.13   The appointment is normally only effective when it has been made by the authorised person, notified to the other party and accepted by the arbitrator. The arbitrator will usually agree the fee basis before accepting, which could be hourly, daily, lump sum, or a mixture of these. In an appointment made by the RIBA the appointment is not confirmed until accepted by the arbitrator. However with some institutions, in particular the RICS, the appointment may be valid from the day it is made by the institution.

4.14   The Act makes provision for the court to adjust the arbitrator's fees in cases of dispute (*see 8.23*) and as the arbitrator is under a duty to avoid unnecessary expense, no arbitrator would be able to treat an appointment as a blank cheque to run up excessive invoices (*see 5.02*). However if the parties have a maximum ceiling in mind they should make this clear to the appointing institution or the arbitrator as appropriate at the outset.

Staying legal proceedings

4.15   A party to an arbitration agreement against whom legal proceedings
are brought may apply to the court for a stay with respect to any
matter which under the agreement should be referred to arbitration
(S.9(1)). The court must grant the stay unless it is satisfied that the
arbitration agreement is 'null and void, inoperative or incapable of
being performed' (S.9(4)). The application may be made even if
arbitration is not to take place until after some other form of dispute
resolution has been exhausted (S.9(2)). A stay may be brought with
respect to part only of legal proceedings, if the arbitration agreement
covers only part of the dispute.

4.16   Where there is a dispute about whether the matter which is the subject
of the action is one covered by the arbitration agreement, this dispute
itself could be referred to arbitration, as the arbitrator would have the
power to decide this question under Section 30, unless the parties have
agreed otherwise (*see 5.24*). However it is arguable that in some
circumstances the court would not be obliged to grant a stay, as
Section 30 does not give the arbitrator exclusive jurisdiction to decide
such disputes.

4.17   The application for a stay must be made to the court in which the
proceedings have been brought, after acknowledging the legal
proceedings, but either before taking any step in those proceedings
(S.9(3)) or simultaneously with the first step. A notice must be sent to
the other party.

4.18   Under Section 86 of the Act, which has not been implemented, the
court was given a discretion to stay legal proceedings with respect to
domestic arbitrations in a wider range of circumstances than those
under Section 9(4). The Section corresponded in substance to the
position which had existed prior to the Act, set out in Section 4 of the
Arbitration Act 1950. As Section 86 has not been brought into force,
the court is now obliged to grant a stay in all but exceptional
circumstances. What has in effect been a removal of the court's
discretion has been much criticised, and it is worth drawing attention
to some issues that may affect the initial decision to enter into an
arbitration agreement.

4.19   A key area where the court might have exercised its discretion was
where it thought that the arbitration was one which concerned issues
in common with other disputes, and the court's powers of joinder

could result in all the questions being considered together, thus producing overall efficacy and fairness. It will no longer be possible to argue that a stay should be refused because the dispute involves parties other than those party to the arbitration agreement. This increases the necessity for having enforceable multi-party arbitration provisions in any arbitration agreement, but even these would only apply in specific circumstances (*see 7.33*), and would not normally cover, for example, the joinder of a claim against a consultant.

4.20   Another area was where only part of the dispute could be referred to arbitration, as the arbitrator's jurisdiction did not cover all the issues raised. The court might consider it inefficient for the same dispute to be heard by more than one tribunal, something that could lead to anomalous results. (For a full discussion see *Mustill and Boyd*, 1989, pp 478–83.) The arbitration agreement must, therefore, be framed broadly enough to cover all possible disputes.

4.21   The court's lack of discretion will also result in difficulties in enforcing adjudicators' decisions (*see 1.17*). If a party fails to comply with an adjudicator's decision, this will constitute a breach of a legal obligation which could give rise to a claim. It had been hoped that an application could be made to the court for immediate judgment under RSC Order 14. However it seems likely that the court's obligation to stay legal proceedings where there is an arbitration agreement may also apply to applications to enforce an adjudicator's decision. This will depend on whether the agreement to arbitrate is expressed broadly enough to cover the obligation to comply with the adjudicator's decision.

4.22   It has been suggested that a possible impasse could be avoided by the parties providing in their contract that adjudicators' decisions will always be enforceable, in spite of any queries or challenges to the decision. Rule 24 of the draft Construction Industry Model Adjudication Procedure, whereby the parties agree that they will be entitled to summary enforcement, and will not raise issues of set-off, counterclaim and abatement, is an example of a provision which aims to achieve this result. Alternatively a statutory instrument could make this provision, but at the time of writing there do not appear to be any such plans.

5   The arbitrator, the parties, the courts

5.01   The Act sets out duties and powers for the arbitrator, the parties and the courts. Once the arbitration has commenced, a complex relationship comes into existence between these three participants. This Chapter explores this triangular relationship by examining the role of each in turn.

Arbitrator's obligations

5.02   The arbitrator's obligations derive from the Act, the agreement to arbitrate, and the terms of the arbitrator's own appointment with the parties. Section 33 of the Act requires that the tribunal shall:
'(a) act fairly and impartially as between the parties, giving each party a reasonable opportunity of putting his case and dealing with that of his opponent; and
(b) adopt procedures suitable to the circumstances of the particular case, avoiding unnecessary delay or expense, so as to provide a fair means for the resolution of the matters falling to be determined'. (S.33(1))

5.03   In addition, other sections of the Act require, either directly or by implication, that the arbitrator :
- is qualified as required by the arbitration agreement (S.24(1)(b));
- is capable of conducting the proceedings (S.24(1)(c));
- does not exceed his or her powers (S.68(2)(b));
- observes agreed procedures (S.68(2)(c));
- deals with all the issues raised in the arbitration (S.68(2)(d)).

5.04   The two obligations in Section 33 are interrelated and link closely with the general principles set out in Section 1 of the Act (*see 2.11*). Acting fairly and reasonably between the parties is of paramount importance, but the obligation to adopt suitable procedures makes it absolutely clear that there is no requirement to mimic court procedures; in fact in certain situations these might be entirely unsuitable. It is also made clear that the arbitrator is only required to allow each party a reasonable opportunity to present his or her case. The requirement to avoid unnecessary delay is underlined by Section 24 which, by implication, requires that the arbitrator should use all reasonable dispatch in conducting the proceedings (S.24(d)(ii)). The arbitrator is also given the freedom and power to adopt a strict approach to parties who are slow to respond or dilatory in any way.

5.05   The arbitrator will need to steer a careful course to fulfill both these
obligations, as it is difficult to ensure simultaneously that both parties
are treated fairly and at the same time keep the proceedings moving
with reasonable speed. In situations where the parties insist, against
the advice of the arbitrator, on pursuing a slow and expensive course,
the arbitrator may either give way to their requests, in which case they
would not be in a position to complain of a breach of Section 33, or
possibly resign.

5.06   The Act requires that the arbitrator should be impartial, but does not
specifically state that the arbitrator must be independent. Someone
with a past or current link with one of the parties is not precluded
from acting, provided they can maintain their impartiality. However
where the link may raise 'justifiable doubts as to his impartiality'
(S.24(1)(a)), an arbitrator should seriously consider whether to take
on or continue with the reference. For practical reasons, no one with
even a distant link with the subject matter of the dispute should act, in
case they are required as a witness (*see 5.20*).

Arbitrator's fees

5.07   The parties are jointly and severally liable to the arbitrator for his or
her fees and expenses (S.28(1)). This provision has nothing to do with
how the fees (and other costs) will be apportioned between the parties
(*see 8.11*). Expenses include the cost of legal assessors etc, as provided
by Section 37(2).

5.08   If the parties have agreed terms regarding fees and expenses, they are
bound by these terms (S.28(5)). If there is no such agreement, they are
nevertheless liable for the arbitrator's reasonable fees and expenses.
Where one party has agreed terms with the arbitrator but the other
has not, the second would be liable for any reasonable fees and
expenses, and the first would have to make up any excess (*Harris,
Planterose et al, p124*). Under Section 28(2), any party may apply to
the court, who may direct that the arbitrator's fees and expenses may
be considered and adjusted by any means it decides are appropriate
(*see also 8.23*).

Arbitrator's immunity

5.09   Section 29 of the Act states :
'An arbitrator is not liable for anything done or omitted in the
discharge or purported discharge of his functions as an arbitrator
unless the act or omission is shown to have been in bad faith.'
(S.29(1))

5.10   This is a mandatory section, which cannot be contravened by
agreement between the parties. It will be up to the courts to interpret
the exception, ie whether 'bad faith' will necessarily involve a moral
element. The immunity will not cover the liability an arbitrator may
incur by resigning (S.29(3)). In other words if the arbitrator resigns,
this could constitute a breach of his or her contract with the parties,
and the immunity does not prevent them from bringing a claim
against the arbitrator for any losses they suffer as a result of this
breach. The court has the power to grant the arbitrator relief from
this liability if it thinks it was reasonable for the arbitrator to resign
(S.25).

Powers of the arbitrator

5.11   The arbitrator's powers derive from the Act and from the agreement
of the parties, including any rules incorporated by reference. The Act
has given the arbitrator a very wide range of powers, which are listed
in Table 3. Some of these are new and serve to strengthen the position
of the arbitrator. All of them are subject to the agreement of the
parties and therefore may be restricted or enlarged as the reference
progresses.

5.12   JCT 80 clause 41.4 expressly gives the arbitrator the following powers:

·   To rectify the contract so that it accurately reflects the true
    agreement between the parties.
    (Provided for under Section 48(5)(c) of the Act, unless otherwise
    agreed by the parties.)
·   To direct such measurements and/or valuations as may be desirable
    to determine the rights of the parties and ascertain any sum due.
    (Provided for under Section 37(1)(a) of the Act, unless otherwise
    agreed by the parties.)
·   'To open up, review or revise any certificate, opinion, decision ...
    requirement or notice and to determine all matters in dispute which

shall be submitted to him in the same manner as if no certificate, opinion, decision, requirement or notice had been given.'

5.13   This last express power has been the subject of much debate. Identical wording led the court in the 1985 case of *Northern Regional Health Authority v Derek Crouch Construction Company* to state that the court had no such power. This meant in effect that they had no power to replace the decision of the architect with their own, by determining whether or not he or she had reached the right answer, but simply to determine whether the decision had been made in the correct manner (ie at the right time, in the correct form). This decision has been much discussed and criticised, but has not been overruled. (For a recent example of judicial consideration of *Crouch* see the case of *Tarmac Construction Limited v Esso Petroleum Limited*, 1996. For an analysis of both *Crouch* and *Tarmac* see *Wallace*, 1997b). The decision in itself is something to be borne in mind when drawing up an agreement to arbitrate. The Courts and Legal Services Act 1990 now allows the parties to confer on the judge the same powers as an arbitrator might have.

Table 3. Powers of the Arbitrator

Subject	*Section*
To rule on its own substantive jurisdiction	30–31
To decide all procedural and evidential matters	34 (1)
To appoint experts and assessors	37
To order a claimant to provide security for the costs of the arbitration	38(3)
To give directions in relation to property	38(4)
To direct that a party or a witness be examined on oath	38(5)
To give directions for the preservation of evidence'	38(6)
To make provisional awards	39(1)
To make an award dismissing the claim	41(3) and (6)
To continue in the absence of one party	41(4)
To make peremptory orders	41(5)
To give directions for failure to comply with a peremptory order	41(7)
To decide cases by principles other than the law	46
To make interim awards	47
To award various remedies	48
To award simple and compound interest	49
To correct awards, and make additional awards	57
To award costs	61
To limit recoverable costs	65

5.14 Rule 12 of the JCT 1988 Arbitration Rules also expressly confers powers on the arbitrator:
· to take legal and technical advice;
· to give directions for protecting, storing, securing or disposing of property the subject of the dispute;
· to order security for costs;
· to proceed in the absence of one of the parties;
· to determine costs;
· to direct the giving of evidence by affidavit;
· to order the production of documents.

All of these powers are available under the Act (*see Table 3*). Their incorporation in a set of rules adopted by the parties constitutes an agreement that the Arbitrator will have these powers.

Obligations of the parties

5.15 The Act requires the parties to 'do all things necessary for the proper and expeditious conduct of the arbitral proceedings' (S.40(1)). This includes complying without delay with any determinations, orders or directions of the arbitrator (S.40(2)(a)) and taking without delay any necessary steps to obtain a decision from the court on a preliminary question of law or jurisdiction (S.40(2)(b)). This is one of the mandatory sections and cannot be avoided by agreement. It is given force by the powers of the arbitrator under Sections 41 and 42.

Rights of the parties

5.16 The rights of the parties are set out in Table 4. The Act allows the parties the freedom to make agreements over provisions, apart from those set out in Schedule 1 (*see Table 1*). The Act deliberately sets out to emphasise party autonomy and the flexibility of arbitration, setting up a framework whereby the parties may tailor the arbitration to suit their needs. As discussed under Chapter 3, this is often best done in the original arbitration agreement. Where circumstances change during the arbitration the parties will have a choice of trying to persuade the other party to agree amendment to the provisions, or be subject to the direction of the arbitrator.

Table 4. Rights of the parties as set out in the Act

Subject	Section
To apply for a stay if other party litigates	9
To apply for an order to extend time	12
To agree matters concerning the appointment of the arbitrator	15–18, 20–22, 25, 27
To revoke the authority of the arbitrator	23
To apply to the court to determine arbitrator's fees	28
To object to the arbitrator's jurisdiction	31
To make agreement with other party on a range of matters including:	
Most convenient venue for hearing	34(a)
Form of pleadings	34(c)
Effect of and limitation of discovery	34(d)
Whether full oral hearing necessary	34(e)
Matters of evidence	34(f) and (h)
Whether arbitrator should have inquisitorial powers	34(g)
Powers and jurisdiction of arbitrator, including those in the case of a party's default	30, 37–39, 41
To ask for consolidation	35
To be represented at the hearing	36
To decide whether provisional award required	39
To take no part	41, 72
To determine powers of the court in relation to the arbitration	42–45
To decide matters in relation to the award	48–49, 52–55, 58
To agree matters concerning costs	63–65
To challenge the award	67, 68
To appeal on a point of law	69

The court's powers

5.17   The court can only influence the course of an arbitration on the request of a party; it has no absolute right to interfere. The Act gives it a limited range of powers, shown in Table 5.

Removal of the arbitrator

5.18   Unless otherwise agreed the authority of the arbitrator may not be revoked except by the parties acting jointly, or by a third party or body given that power by the parties (S.23(3)). This provision is new; prior to the Act the authority of the arbitrator could only be revoked

Table 5. The court's powers as conferred by the Act

Subject	Section
To extend time for beginning proceedings	12, 13, 79
To appoint arbitrators	18, 21
To remove the arbitrator	24
To grant relief to arbitrator on resignation	25
To determine arbitrator's fees	28
To determine preliminary point of jurisdiction	32
To enforce a peremptory order	42
To subpoena a witnesses	43
To take the evidence of witnesses	44(2)(a)
To preserve evidence	44(2)(b)
To authorise the entering of premises for inspection and taking of samples	44(2)(c)
To order the sale of goods	44(2)(d)
To grant an interim injunction or the appointment of a receiver	44(2)(e)
To determine of preliminary point of law	45
To extend time for the making of an award	50
To assess the arbitrator's fees	56
To determine costs	63
To enforce an award	66
To confirm, vary or set aside an award	67, 68
To determine of a question of law arising out of an award	69

with the leave of the High Court unless the agreement stated to the contrary. The parties are free to agree the circumstances of the revocation, and in practice these are likely to come under any procedural rules adopted. The revocation must be in writing unless the parties also agree to terminate the arbitration agreement. This exception is inserted for practical reasons: where the parties mutually allow an arbitration agreement to lapse they will not have put this agreement into writing – accordingly there is no requirement to put the revocation of the arbitrator's authority in writing.

5.19   Where only one party wishes the removal of the arbitrator, it may also apply to the court under Section 24, provided that it has given notice to the other party (S.80), and provided it has exhausted any possible methods available through other institutions or persons who may be invested with such power (eg an appointing body). The grounds for an application are:
 ·   impartiality;
 ·   lack of qualifications;

- physical or mental incapability of conducting the proceedings;
- failure or refusal to properly conduct the proceedings, or failure to conduct them with reasonable speed to the extent that substantial injustice will be caused (S.24).

5.20   It should be noted that lack of independence is not a ground on its own, provided of course that this has no effect on the arbitrator's impartiality. For example, an arbitrator may frequently have had past or current business relations with one or other of the parties, or may be associated with the legal representative of one of the parties, a situation not uncommon in the closely knit circles of construction litigation, but this connection would not per se be sufficient to remove the arbitrator.

5.21   The grounds of failure or refusal properly to conduct the proceedings, or failure to conduct them with reasonable speed to the extent that substantial injustice will be caused, relate closely to the arbitrator's obligations under Section 33, but it should be noted that the applicant must also show that such failure will cause injustice to the applicant.

5.22   The arbitrator has the right to present his or her case to the court, and the court upon removal may give directions regarding fees, etc. The arbitrator also has the right to continue with the arbitration, though it may be unwise to do so unless the challenge is entirely on spurious grounds. After removal, the court may make an order as to the payment or repayment of fees and expenses (S.24(4)). If the parties cannot agree on a replacement, or any appointing institution fails to make an appointment, then the provisions of Sections 17 and 18 (court appointment of arbitrators) will apply.

Resignation of the arbitrator

5.23   An arbitrator's right to resign will depend on the terms of his or her appointment. The Act itself provides no right, but provides for the consequences of a resignation, as long as the parties have agreed nothing to the contrary (S.25). An arbitrator who resigns may, if the method of determining fees has not been agreed with the parties, apply to the court for an order. The court will only grant relief where it considers it has been reasonable for the arbitrator to resign; for example where the arbitrator is unhappy with procedures being insisted on by the parties (there may be a conflict with the duties under Section 33), or where the arbitration may have taken a course entirely different from that envisaged at the time of appointment. Where the resignation is in a good cause, the court may grant relief from any liability incurred (*see 5.10*). If the parties have not agreed how the vacancy may be filled, the provisions of Sections 16 and 18 would apply.

Objections to the arbitration

5.24   Sections 31 and 32 of the Act provide means of making objections to the jurisdiction of the arbitrator during the course of the arbitration: Section 31 by means of raising an objection with the arbitrator, and Section 32 through the court. Any objection that the arbitrator lacks authority to hear the dispute at all, ie that he or she lacks substantive jurisdiction, must be made at the start of the proceedings (S.31(1)). Any objection that the arbitrator is dealing with matters with which he or she has no specific authority to deal, ie that the arbitrator is exceeding his or her jurisdiction, must be raised as soon as possible, and before any steps with respect to the matter objected have been taken (S.31(2)). Both these qualifications are likely to be interpreted according to what is reasonable in the particular circumstances. The arbitrator has the power to extend the period for either objection where it seems appropriate (S.31(3)). However if any party delays raising the question for an unjustifiable period of time, Section 73 of the Act makes it clear that the party may lose the right to object entirely.

5.25   Once an objection under Section 31 has been raised, two things may happen. First, the arbitrator may make a ruling as to his or her own jurisdiction (S.31(4)). The arbitrator will do this in the form of an award, either in a separate award on jurisdiction, or in the final award. The former is more likely, particularly if the objection is raised early in the arbitration. The arbitrator may hold a special hearing as soon as possible to deal with this specific question. Either party has the power to appeal this award (*see 8.30*). If the question is decided in the final award, the objecting party has three choices. He or she may resist an application to enforce the award on the grounds of lack of jurisdiction of the award (*see 8.27*); challenge the award on the grounds of lack of jurisdiction (*see 8.28*); or appeal the award on the question of jurisdiction (*see 8.30*).

5.26   Secondly, the arbitrator may allow a stay so that the court can consider the question (S.31(5)). The court's power to decide a question of jurisdiction is a mandatory provision, but it is unlikely to be used where the arbitrator has such power. It will of course be the only course of action available where the arbitrator does not have power to rule on his or her own jurisdiction. The application must satisfy several pre-conditions set out in the Act to be valid. For example, it must comply with the time limits set out in Section 31. An application to the court will not be considered unless it is made jointly by the parties, or with the permission of the arbitrator (S.32(2)). In the latter case the court must also be satisfied that there is likely to be a substantial saving in costs, and that there is good reason why the matter should be decided by the court. While the court is considering the jurisdiction question, the arbitrator has a discretion whether to continue with the arbitration, unless the parties agree that the proceedings should be stayed. An arbitrator would generally be wise to do this unless the arbitration is likely to be short and the challenge appears to have little validity (*University of Reading v Miller Construction Ltd*, 1994).

6 Procedures before the hearing

6.01   The Act lays down very few procedural requirements, and with the
         exception of the obligation on the arbitrator to act fairly and
         expeditiously, all other requirements are subject to the agreement of
         the parties. A very wide variety of procedures is therefore possible,
         from extremely short and informal arbitrations to lengthy processes
         almost indistinguishable from court proceedings. The courts have
         tolerated and supported this wide variety, provided always that the
         proceedings followed the agreement of the parties.

6.02   It is nevertheless useful to describe a range of possible procedures so
         that the reader has an approximate idea of what to expect.
         Construction arbitrations have always tended to fall into a narrower
         range of forms than might be found in commodity or shipping
         arbitrations, due perhaps to the complex and technical nature of the
         disputes, and the preferences and habits of the arbitrators and the
         parties' legal advisors. This narrower range is reflected in the 1988
         JCT Arbitration Rules which, though currently under revision, form a
         useful starting point as they set out three model procedures which
         serve to illustrate the range. These three procedures are:
         ·   Rule 5: procedure without a hearing;
         ·   Rule 6: full procedure with a hearing;
         ·   Rule 7: short procedure with a hearing.

Procedure without a hearing

6.03   The arbitrator makes an award on documentary evidence only. There
         are provisions for the parties serving statements of claim, defence,
         counterclaim, reply to the defence, defence to the counterclaim and
         reply to the defence to the counterclaim (*see 6.16*). With these
         statements the parties are required to submit a list of relevant
         documents and a copy of any document on which they seek to rely.
         The arbitrator then makes an award on the basis of the documentary
         evidence. If appropriate the arbitrator may also inspect the site.

6.04   'Documents only' arbitrations are less popular in construction than
         they are in other areas, such as shipping, and less popular in the UK
         than in other European countries. In the UK the legal professions
         generally prefer an oral hearing. However, unless documentary
         evidence is scanty, very considerable savings in cost can be achieved
         by avoiding a full hearing. The cost of renting premises, the daily
         rates of solicitors and barristers for attendance, the loss of earnings by
         the parties and the witnesses are all likely to be extremely high, so

serious consideration should be given to whether a documents only arbitration would be acceptable. Once the dispute has arisen it is easy to get into the frame of mind where an opportunity to 'say one's bit' and question in detail the opponent's case can seem essential, but a competent arbitrator can assess a great deal from written submissions plus documents. If certain points appear unclear the arbitrator can always raise them with the parties and suggest a short meeting at which he or she questions the parties on those specific matters.

Full procedure with a hearing

6.05   This involves the parties serving statements of claim, defence, counterclaim, reply to the defence, defence to the counterclaim and reply to the defence to the counterclaim, as in Rule 5, but with the addition of an oral hearing. Details of how the procedure might work in practice before the hearing and the forms the oral hearing might take are discussed below and in Chapter 7.

Short procedure with a hearing

6.06   The short procedure is only suitable for simpler disputes. The timescales are extremely short: a hearing takes place within 21 days of the decision to adopt Rule 7; all documents to be relied on are exchanged seven days before the hearing; and the arbitrator should publish the award within seven days of the hearing. The entire process, therefore, is concluded within 28 days. This has been criticised as being unrealistically short.

6.07   The rather short time frames set out under the JCT Rules has made them unpopular with some arbitrators and parties, and had led to them being 'un-agreed' at the commencement of many arbitrations. However it is understood that some of the time frames are being lengthened in the new Rules. Also, the requirement that the arbitrator should act expeditiously may give added incentive to following the JCT Rules.

Deciding on the procedure to be adopted

6.08   Section 34 of the Act states that 'It shall be for the tribunal to decide all procedural and evidential matters, subject to the right of the parties to agree any matter,' and gives a non-exhaustive list of what procedural and evidential matters may include. This gives the widest discretion to the parties to agree any procedure that they prefer, either in advance or during the arbitration, and the arbitrator must always give effect to their agreement. Where they cannot agree, the arbitrator has absolute power to direct them, and this power should be exercised in accordance with his or her mandatory duty under Section 33. This power is confirmed in Rule 4 of the JCT Arbitration Rules which expressly gives the arbitrator the power to decide on which Rule should be followed, should the parties fail to agree.

6.09   The list of matters given in Section 34(2) is indicative of the wide range of issues which the parties may determine by agreement:
- time and place of any proceedings, including the hearing;
- written statements of claim and defence (*see 6.16*): it is possible to keep these very brief and informal should the parties prefer – in fact the Act makes it clear that it is acceptable to dispense with any pleadings whatsoever;
- documents (*see 6.22*): again the Act makes it quite clear that there is no requirement to follow a formal discovery process;
- evidence (*see 7.13*): the Act makes it clear that the strict rules of evidence need not be followed;
- inquisitorial procedures: this process, whereby the arbitrator makes his own inquiries, is somewhat alien to those used in common law tradition, but the Act makes it clear that the arbitrator has this power. In certain circumstances, for example where the arbitrator has particular expertise, investigating the issue himself may well be consistent with the arbitrator's obligation to proceed economically and expeditiously;
- oral hearing: if only one party wishes an oral hearing, it will be for the arbitrator to decide whether such a hearing is necessary. This is not in fact an 'all or nothing' situation; if the arbitrator thinks it appropriate, a hearing may be held on only some of the issues.

6.10   The arbitrator will advise the parties about suitable procedures if they have not already agreed the procedure they wish to adopt. In some complex construction disputes detailed and lengthy procedures may be essential to achieve an accurate and just outcome. But they would be inappropriate in the case of a simple dispute involving a relatively small sum of money. Frequently the parties in the heat of the dispute, perhaps encouraged by their legal advisors, demand protracted and detailed proceedings under the impression that otherwise they may not be able to present their case fully. Achieving an appropriate balance requires a skilled arbitrator and parties who appreciate the possibilities which are available, and are reasonably open to suggestion. There is little that the arbitrator can do to keep proceedings short and simple in the face of joint requests from the parties tending to the contrary. Agreeing procedural matters in advance can avoid this problem (*see Chapter 3*).

Preliminary meeting

6.11   It is usual to hold a preliminary meeting with both parties and their representatives. The basis of the arbitration, including the agreement, the appointment, and the matters to be referred, are confirmed and if necessary clarified, and various procedural matters discussed.

6.12   Frequently there is a secondary result. This meeting may be the first occasion on which the parties have met for some time, and as it becomes apparent during the course of the meeting the seriousness of the position they have reached and the length and expense of the arbitration stretching before them, they often decide to settle their differences shortly after the meeting (*see 8.07*).

6.13   The arbitrator will usually have a full checklist of all the matters that need to be resolved either by the parties' agreement or the arbitrator's determination, which may be issued as an agenda before the meeting. These may include:
    ·   Whether jurisdiction is challenged
        It is important that any question as to jurisdiction is dealt with as early as possible, and the arbitrator is likely to raise the issue himself (*see 5.24*).
    ·   Procedural matters
        This may be simply a matter of confirming which set of procedural rules apply (*see 6.02*).
    ·   Particular powers, including appointment of legal assessor, ability to order security for costs, the making of provisional awards, inquisitorial powers etc (*see 5.11*).
    ·   Interlocutory proceedings: initial meetings, directions, pleadings, discovery, preparation of documents, Scott Schedules (*see 6.25*), experts' reports.
    ·   Matters of evidence and whether strict rules apply (*see 7.13*).

6.14   Other more practical matters may be discussed at the preliminary meeting. It is important to establish the exact identity of each party, and who is bringing the claim. This party will be termed the 'claimant' throughout the proceedings, and the other the 'respondent'. It is also useful to outline the scope of areas in dispute at this stage. This will give the arbitrator an indication of such matters as how long the hearing is likely to take and whether or not advice will be needed. It may even be possible to agree dates, location and timetable for the hearing. The arbitrator may also wish to establish whether the parties will be engaging solicitors or barristers (*see 7.04*), whether a site visit will be needed (*see 7.17*), and whether transcripts or tape recordings will be needed (*see 7.18*). He or she will also wish to establish whether there will be a hearing to consider costs, or whether sealed offers will be handed in at particular stages (*see 7.21*).

Directions

6.15   Following the preliminary meeting the arbitrator will usually give directions regarding various preliminary matters that need to be sorted out prior to the hearing. Sometimes a formal document is issued headed 'Order for Directions'. An example of an Order for Directions is given as Figure 3. There is no appeal procedure for a party against the Order for Directions; the arbitrator's decision on these matters is final.

Pleadings

6.16   'Pleadings' is the term used for the documents in which the parties set out their claims and the facts which they intend to prove and on which they will rely. In an arbitration under the JCT Arbitration Rules the claimant states his or her claim in a document entitled 'Statement of Claim' and the respondent answers the claim in a 'Statement of Defence' (sometimes referred to as 'Points of Claim' and 'Points of Defence'). If there is a counterclaim the document will be a 'Statement of Defence and Counterclaim'. The claimant may then respond with a 'Reply to the Defence', which are further allegations in response to the defence and, where there is a counterclaim, a 'Defence to Counterclaim'. Finally the respondent may submit a 'Reply to the Defence to the Counterclaim'. Occasionally further pleadings will be delivered.

Figure 3. Specimen Order for Directions

In the matter of the Arbitration Act 1996

In the matter of the arbitration between:
    (Claimant's name)   Claimant
    (Respondent's name)   Respondent

ORDER FOR DIRECTIONS

Upon hearing the parties' representations on both sides the following Directions are given:

1   There be pleadings in this arbitration as follows:
- The Claimant shall deliver a statement of case within 28 days of the date of this order.
- The Respondent shall deliver a statement of defence (and of counterclaim if any) to be delivered within 28 days thereafter.
- The Claimant shall deliver a statement of reply to the defence (and of defence to the counterclaim, if any) within 14 days thereafter.
- The Respondent shall deliver a statement of reply to the defence to the counterclaim, if any, within 14 days thereafter.

    Pleadings shall be deemed closed 7 days thereafter.

2   Each of the statements referred to above shall include a list of any documents the Claimant or Respondent as the case may be considers necessary to support any part of the relevant statement, together with a copy of the principal documents on which reliance shall be placed identifying clearly in each document the relevant part or parts on which reliance will be placed.

3   That figures shall be agreed as figures where possible, and that correspondence, photographs and plans be agreed where possible.

4   That a copy of any communication sent to me by either party shall be sent simultaneously to the other party, the original being marked to indicate such copy has been sent.

5   That the hearing of this arbitration is provisionally arranged to commence at (time) on (date), and is estimated to last 4 days. The hearing shall take place at (address).

6   There shall be no more than one expert to each side.

7   That by consent the Claimants shall arrange for a transcript of the hearing to be taken and one copy of such transcript to be prepared for my use. The costs of the transcription shall be costs in the arbitration.

8   That I shall view the subject matter of the arbitration at (time) on (date) in the presence of representatives of both parties.

9   That there shall be liberty to apply.

10 That the costs of this application shall be costs in the arbitration.

Fit for Counsel   (signed) Arbitrator

6.17   A counterclaim differs from a defence in that it will raise a new issue. For example, if an employer claims for defective work the respondent may, in the response, claim that the work is not defective; this would be a defence. The respondent may further claim direct loss and/or expense due to delays caused by the employer; this would be a counterclaim.

6.18   The process may be much simplified by the arbitrator asking the parties to set out their cases in the form of a letter with relevant key documents attached, but even here the Claim-Defence-Reply sequence is usually followed.

6.19   If a party cannot deliver a pleading on time, it should seek the other party's agreement to an extension, and inform the arbitrator of the outcome. If this is not forthcoming the party will have to apply to the arbitrator. If a pleading does not give sufficient detail the other party may ask for clarification, sometimes referred to as 'further and better particulars'. This might occur for example if a pleading referred to a letter without giving its date, or a meeting without saying who was present, or to defects without specifying exactly what the defects were. Occasionally these can be used as a delaying tactic. The other party is not obliged to reply, unless the arbitrator makes an order to that effect.

6.20   Further particulars are sometimes asked for in the form of 'interrogatories'. These are a series of questions, for which there is perhaps little documentary evidence available, to be put to the other party and answered on oath. Interrogatories are rarely required in arbitration.

6.21   The arbitrator will usually read through pleadings when they arrive, and may draw the parties' attention to any errors or discrepancies discovered. All matters to be claimed must be set out in the pleadings. New claims cannot be raised later without the other party's or the arbitrator's agreement. The arbitrator may grant a party leave to amend pleadings at any stage, and normally will allow all amendments which are necessary to ascertain the real questions between the parties. The only exceptions might be where the arbitrator feels the party has acted in bad faith, or that by an earlier error the party has done some injury to its opponent which could not be compensated by costs. If the proposed amendment means that the other side has wasted time and money dealing with the original pleading, the arbitrator may allow the amendment, but with 'the costs

Figure 4. Specimen Scott Schedule

Item	Location	Defect	Cause	Allegations against the respondents	Drawing reference
1	2	3	4	5	6
a(1)	Below window G12	Blown plaster and damp wall	Damp penetration through gap in cavity tray under cill	Failed to cut trays to correct length	AD/418 rev D

to be borne by that party in any event' (*see 8.11*). Where the pleadings are complex or confused the arbitrator may ask for a list of issues to be agreed by the parties, setting out clearly the points which the arbitrator is to decide. A further preliminary meeting may be necessary to settle the matter between them.

Discovery

6.22   The principle behind the procedure termed 'discovery' is that each party should be fully aware of all documents in the other's possession pertaining to the case. The purpose of the hearing is to ascertain the true facts in the case, and concealment of evidence is not acceptable. Under the JCT Arbitration Rules the parties must include lists of any documents they consider necessary to support their case with their statements of case etc, together with copies of the principal documents on which reliance will be placed.

6.23   Alternatively the process of discovery may be distinct from the pleadings described above. Parties send each other a list of all documents which are or have been in their possession or power, and which they believe to exist. The documents are made available for inspection and copying to the other party. Following this a bundle of agreed documents is prepared, ie documents whose validity is accepted by both parties, usually by their solicitors. The timing and details of this are normally set out in the arbitrator's order for directions. If one party is suspected of concealing a document, the

Figure 4 *Continued*

emedial work cessary	Amount claimed	Amount (if any) admitted by respondent	Respondent's comments	Arbitrator's comments
	8	9	10	11
emove window, l and top urse, both leaves. t new cavity tray d rebuild. t new window. emove blown ister and repair.	£1,000			

arbitrator may ask it to prepare a fresh list in the form of an affidavit or oath.

6.24   Documents between a party and its solicitor concerning the arbitration are deemed 'privileged', and do not have to be produced at the hearing. Similarly any offers to settle are privileged (*see 7.21*). Sometimes such letters are headed 'without prejudice', but the heading itself is not sufficient or even necessary to render the document privileged; it is the purpose and content which determines whether it must be produced.

Scott Schedule

6.25   These documents present the claim and defence in tabular form, referring back to the original documents (*see Fig 4*). They are particularly useful where the dispute covers a large number of smaller issues, as is common in complex construction cases, and where there have been numerous requests for further and better particulars. The document summarises all the issues in a clear and accessible manner, rather than having them scattered throughout numerous other pleadings. It also focuses the parties' minds on the points of agreement and of difference.

6.26   In the example of a Scott Schedule shown in Figure 4 the claimant would normally prepare the Schedule and complete columns 1–8. The Schedule would then be sent to the respondent who would complete columns 9 and 10. The last column is left for the arbitrator's own use. The Schedule may be cross referenced to separate schedules if this is more concise, for example where there are large numbers of similar defects across a housing scheme. It is normally completed after discovery, and it is quite likely that the arbitrator may wish to look through it prior to the hearing.

Expert witnesses

6.27   When disputes involve matters of technical complexity the parties often engage expert witnesses. The arbitrator may also appoint experts (*see 7.06*). On smaller disputes there is rarely more than one expert appointed by each side, but on large disputes four a side or even more is possible.

6.28   Expert witnesses are practitioners considered expert in a particular technical area who give their opinion about the facts of the case and current industry standards in order to assist the arbitrator. For example, they might give evidence as to what is generally considered an acceptable standard of workmanship, and whether it has been reached in that particular case. Their opinion should be given objectively and contained within their own area of expertise, without seeking to polarise issues or act as advocates for their side. They should state the facts and assumptions upon which their opinion is based, without omitting facts which could detract from their concluded opinion. If at any stage the expert changes his or her mind then this should be notified to the other side and, when appropriate, to the arbitrator.

6.29   Experts generally meet before the hearing, sometimes with the arbitrator, in order to try and agree as many matters as possible and narrow the areas of dispute. Meetings of experts (normally of like discipline) are ordered by the arbitrator and are on a without prejudice basis. They are not attended by legal advisors, and are normally convened and hosted by the claimant's expert. Matters which may be agreed are matters of fact, and sometimes of opinion on the less contentious issues. For example, quantity surveyors may be able to agree on the value of remedial work carried out, though they may not agree on its necessity or its success. The experts' evidence is usually given in the form of reports which are finalised and exchanged following this meeting.

7   Form and conduct of the hearing

7.01   The procedures during the hearing can be as varied as those which precede it. On smaller disputes the hearing may be brief and informal, and last only a few days; on large complex disputes it may last for several weeks and follow a pattern close to that of a court hearing. The parties have the right to agree the form the proceedings will take; if they cannot agree, the arbitrator has the power to decide on their behalf (S.34(1)).

7.02   Hearings are always private, with the public and press excluded. The arbitrator will fix the time, date and venue of the hearing, with the parties' agreement. Normally the hearing will take place on 'neutral territory', ie accommodation specially hired for the purpose. For shorter arbitrations however, the hearing may take place at the premises of one of the parties or the arbitrator.

Documents to be provided

7.03   Four bundles of agreed documents, and other documents on which each party will rely (*see 6.22*), are usually required by the arbitrator for the hearing: one for the arbitrator, one for each party, and one for the witnesses. The arbitrator will not normally examine the documents in detail prior to a hearing, but may inspect the general layout of the files. If a party fails to produce a document, or to give evidence, the other party may apply to the High Court with the permission of the arbitrator or other party (S.43(1)).

Legal representation

7.04   Unless the parties otherwise agree, a party may be represented by a lawyer or other person (S.36). Parties generally engage a solicitor. However if a party wishes to engage a barrister ('Counsel') it should inform the arbitrator and the other party.

7.05   Where there is no legal representation, there will be no formal pleadings as discussed above. Generally each party will submit a short statement to the arbitrator, who will then hold a hearing where the parties will expand on their case, and the arbitrator will question each party.

Expert witnesses, advisors, assessors

7.06   The appointment of experts by the parties is discussed under 6.27. In addition the Act states that unless otherwise agreed by the parties, the arbitrator may also appoint experts, legal advisors or assessors, and the costs are expenses of the arbitrator for the purposes of the Act (S.37). This may overcome some of the difficulties raised earlier in connection with the tendency for experts to act as advocates for their clients, and also produce a considerable saving in cost. The arbitrator must give the parties opportunity to consider the advice or information given, but can limit the time spent, for example, by requiring any party appointed expert to respond in writing. The arbitrator may take legal advice on preliminary points before the hearing, but cannot substitute that advice for his or her own decision.

7.07   Expert evidence is usually given in reports exchanged before the hearing and where it is agreed that there is no need for oral evidence. Where a party wishes to challenge the expert evidence it will generally be allowed to cross-examine the expert witness at the hearing.

Procedure

7.08   The procedure may vary, but typically is as follows:
   · claimant's opening statement (including defence to counterclaim)
   · claimant calls witnesses
   · examination in chief
   · cross examination
   · re-examination
   · respondent's opening statement (defence and counterclaim)
   · respondent calls witnesses
   · examination in chief
   · cross examination
   · re-examination
   · respondent's closing statement
   · claimant's closing statement
   · arbitrator formally closes the hearing.

   If the respondent has admitted the claimant's case subject to a counterclaim, then the order will be reversed.

7.09   The arbitrator's questions to witnesses should be asked after re-examination, after which both parties may ask further questions on the points that have been raised. Before the closing statements, the arbitrator may ask the parties to address particular points of interest, but the arbitrator will not normally express views at this stage.

Witnesses

7.10   Evidence is normally given on oath or affirmation. With an oath, this would be taken on the appropriate religious book, in the manner in which the witness considers binding according to his or her religion. Affirmation may be used when the witness objects to being sworn on oath, or where it is impractical to do so. The Oaths Act 1978 sets out the following affirmation:
'I (name) do solemnly, sincerely and truly declare and affirm that the evidence I shall give shall be the truth, the whole truth and nothing but the truth.'

7.11   Architects are frequently called as witnesses in disputes between employer and contractor. Attendance is obligatory, as a party to an arbitration may use the same procedures as those available to a court to secure the attendance of witnesses, provided the witness is in the United Kingdom (S.43). However the flexibility of arbitration means that dates can usually be arranged which are not seriously inconvenient.

7.12   Normally the party's legal advisors or, if there are none, the arbitrator, will advise the witnesses as to procedure, though they are not coached or rehearsed in the way they would be in the United States. All answers should be addressed to the arbitrator, and witnesses should focus on giving the facts as they remember them, and refrain from giving opinion. If they cannot remember events clearly they should say so. Witnesses should respond from memory but may refer to contemporaneous writing if necessary, which should always be shown to the arbitrator and the other party.

Evidence

7.13   The rules of evidence are extremely complex, and the parties are free to agree that the arbitrator need not follow them strictly. With respect to any claim made the rule is 'he who asserts must prove' and the claim must be proved beyond the balance of probability. In other words, the arbitrator must conclude that it is more likely than not that the fact asserted is true. Some of the more important rules of evidence are:

- evidence must be relevant to the facts in issue;
- evidence must be admissible in law;
- leading questions are only permitted in cross-examination (except for non-contentious issues);
- questions testing accuracy and credibility are allowed during cross-examination;
- oral evidence of the contents of a document is not acceptable – the document itself must be produced;
- when a document is relied on, the original must usually be produced;
- 'hearsay' evidence is now generally admissible (*see Glossary*).

7.14   Section 34(2)(f) gives the arbitrator wide powers to decide what evidence to admit and what weight to attach to it. It allows the arbitrator, for example, to disregard the hearsay rule, or to admit the written statements of witnesses who are unable to attend. In such circumstances the arbitrator would have to be careful to avoid injustice to the other party.

7.15   If there has been an adjudication prior to the arbitration, the adjudicator may be called as a witness, unless the parties have agreed that he or she may not be called, as stipulated, for example, in the Construction Industry Model Adjudication Procedure rule 27, or unless the adjudicator has excluded this possibility under the terms of appointment. If the adjudicator is called, although able to give direct evidence of events, for example of a site visit made at the time of the adjudication, any evidence of what was said during the adjudication proceedings would be hearsay, and it will be up to the arbitrator to decide how much weight to give it. The arbitrator is also likely to be aware of the decision of the adjudicator. However this decision is not evidence of the truth of the facts which it sets out, and it would normally be open to the arbitrator to reach the opposite conclusion.

7.16   An arbitrator will generally not refuse to hear evidence, unless there is good reason to limit it. If a party objects to the evidence being heard it must object at the time; the arbitrator can then hear submissions from both sides and rule as to its admissibility. Hearing evidence to which the other party objects may be considered to show lack of impartiality, and may result in the award being set aside. There may be good reason to limit the evidence if the arbitrator is convinced on a point, but the arbitrator must make it clear why this is being done, in case the opposing party wishes to bring forth further evidence.

Viewing premises

7.17   Frequently arbitrators will view the premises subject of the dispute. This could happen before, during or after the hearing. It is usual for representatives of the parties to accompany the arbitrator, who should not go alone without their permission. The arbitrator will make it clear whether evidence will be accepted during the course of the visit, or whether the view forms no part of the hearing.

Shorthand note/tape recording

7.18   It is the arbitrator's duty to take comprehensive notes. If it is desired to use the services of a court stenographer or shorthand-writer the arbitrator should obtain the parties' agreement to this in advance, including the allocation of the costs. The arbitrator may make a tape of the proceedings to supplement his or her notes.

Determination of a preliminary point of law

7.19   Unless otherwise agreed by the parties, under Section 45 of the Act either party may apply to the court to determine a preliminary point of law. This section is non-mandatory: in other words the parties may agree that the court will have no such jurisdiction. The agreement will be binding whether it is made before or after the commencement of the arbitration, provided it is made in writing. An agreement to dispense with reasons in the award would also be taken as an agreement to exclude this right.

7.20   The application may be made by one party with the permission of all other parties or with the permission of the tribunal. It should state the question of law to be determined and the reasons why the court should determine it. The court will not consider it unless the question substantially affects the rights of one of the parties, its determination is likely to produce a substantial saving in costs and the application has been made without delay (S.45(2)). There is no provision for deciding a question that is of general public importance if it does not substantially affect the rights of a party. The decision of the court is treated as a judgment with respect to the issue of appeal, and no appeal will be heard unless the court considers that it raises a question of general importance or there are special reasons why it should be heard.

Offers

7.21   Often during the course of an arbitration one party may decide that it wishes to make an offer to settle the dispute. It does not, of course, wish a judge or arbitrator to be aware of the amount of the offer, in case this influences the decision. In litigation there is a simple way round this problem: a party can make a payment into court, which the other party can take up at any point, and of which the judge has no knowledge.

7.22   The position is not so simple in arbitration. Though the party making the offer would prefer the arbitrator to be unaware of this, it will nevertheless wish the arbitrator to see the offer before making his or her award as to costs. In arbitration, as in litigation, the losing party normally pays the winner's costs. The principle behind this is that if a party succeeds in the action, even in part, there was clearly a justifiable cause and that party would not have suffered costs if the losing party had met its obligations in the first place. However the position is clearly different if the losing party made an offer greater than or equal to the final amount awarded, which the winning party ignored. Had they accepted it, they would be as well off as they were through continuing with the arbitration. Therefore provided that it can be shown that the losing party acted unreasonably in continuing with the arbitration, all costs incurred following the rejection of the offer are normally awarded to the winner (*see 8.11*).

7.23   The arbitrator therefore needs to know of the offer, the amount, and when it was made before making an award as to costs, but after making the award on the substantive issues. This can be done in two ways. After the date for accepting the offer has passed, the offer may be given to the arbitrator in a sealed envelope, to be opened at the appropriate stage. The arbitrator will be aware during the hearing that an offer has been made, but not of the amount. In order to avoid either party compromising its case the arbitrator may request that both parties produce a sealed envelope at certain stages in the proceedings, which of course may be empty if no offer is made. The sealed offer method is normally only used where no hearing on the issue of costs is planned.

7.24   Alternatively the offer can be headed 'without prejudice save as to costs' (often referred to as a 'Calderbank' offer, after a case of that name). After the hearing the parties can request the arbitrator to reserve his award on costs until after further submissions. After making an interim award on the merits of the claim (*see 8.04*) a hearing will be held at which the parties may address the arbitrator as to costs and at which the offer can be produced, following which the arbitrator publishes the final award. Though the arbitrator will have been aware that the offer was made, as with the sealed offer, he or she will not know the amount and will not be handed the document until the second hearing.

Security for costs

7.25   Section 38(3) of the Act gives the arbitrator the power to order the claimant to provide 'security for costs', unless the parties agree otherwise. This avoids the problem which can arise where the claimant is eventually unsuccessful and it transpires that he or she has no funds to meet the respondent's costs, leaving the respondent out of pocket for defending an unjustified claim. Security is normally provided in the form of a cash payment to a trustee/stakeholder or a guarantee by a parent company or bank.

7.26   This power can only be exercised by the arbitrator, and not by the court, which is a significant change from the position before the Act, where only the court could make such an order. The power also extends to a counterclaimant. It appears from the Act that the arbitrator may make such an order on his or her own initiative, but in practice this is unlikely to happen unless requested by a party.

7.27   The Act gives no guidance as to how the arbitrator's power should be exercised, except for stating that it should not be used merely because the claimant is normally resident outside the UK, or a company formed, managed or controlled outside the UK. Whether or not to make such an order is a very difficult decision with serious consequences, because asking the claimant to provide a substantial sum may prevent it from continuing. Two key issues would have been considered by the courts: the ability of the claimant to pay the costs should the claim fail, which would be assessed by reference to the claimant's accounts and other relevant financial information, and the claimant's likelihood of success.

7.28   The arbitrator will therefore need to make an assessment of the strengths of the claim at an early stage, when this may be very difficult to judge, and having made the decision the arbitrator must remain impartial and not allow the initial decision to influence the award. To add to the complication the arbitrator will need to consider any sealed or Calderbank offers which have been made (*see 7.21*). This may also make it difficult for the arbitrator to remain impartial. Unless the parties have great confidence in the arbitrator they may prefer to raise the question of security for costs with another tribunal, or to agree in advance not to give the arbitrator this power.

Sanctions

7.29   It is often the case that one of the parties, usually the respondent, is unwilling to proceed with the arbitration. The party may participate reluctantly, be late in meeting the orders of the arbitrator, or even fail to appear at all. The Act therefore offers a variety of remedies and sanctions to deal with these situations.

7.30   Unless otherwise agreed by the parties, the arbitrator may make an award dismissing the claim where there is inordinate and inexcusable delay on the part of the claimant, and the delay is likely seriously to prejudice the position of the respondent (S.41(3)). This would cover situations where, for example, the delay is so prolonged that the memory of witnesses will have become significantly inaccurate, or the delay is damaging to the professional position of the respondent.

7.31   The arbitrator may also continue with only one party present (sometimes termed '*ex parte*') when one party without good reason fails to attend (S.41(4)). The arbitrator may even go so far as to make an award. Normally, in the face of non-attendance by a party the arbitrator would take various practical steps to ascertain that there was no misunderstanding or other valid reason for non-attendance before proceeding.

7.32   If a party fails to comply with any order or direction then the arbitrator may make a peremptory order. This repeats the original order, specifying a time for compliance and setting out the consequences for failure to comply (S.41(5)). It has been suggested that in order to avoid any doubt the use of the word 'peremptory' in such an order is advisable, eg 'by way of peremptory order, unless the (claimant/respondent) offers his expert's report for exchange on or before (a certain date) he shall not be entitled to rely on any expert evidence.' (*Harris, Planterose et al. 1996, p171*) If a claimant fails to respond to an order to provide security for costs, the arbitrator may make an award dismissing the claim (S.41(6)). If a party fails to comply with any other order, the arbitrator has a choice of sanctions: to disallow it from relying on material which is the subject of the order; to draw adverse inferences; to proceed to an award without the material which is the subject of the order; or to order that the party pays costs in connection with the noncompliance (S.41(7)).

7.33   As an alternative, either the arbitrator and one party, or both parties by agreement, may make an application for a court order to enforce the peremptory order (S.42). The court must be satisfied that the party has exhausted any available arbitral process for enforcement. This provision allows the arbitrator and the parties to take advantage of the wider powers of compulsion available to the court, eg imposing a fine or imprisonment. However, it is extremely unlikely that these powers would ever be needed in arbitration.

Provisional relief

7.34   The Act makes provision for the arbitrator to grant relief in the form of making a provisional order. This power is only available if the parties have granted it to the arbitrator. Any remedy can be ordered that could be granted in a final award, for example, the respondent can be ordered to pay the claimant a sum of money. The provisional order is subject to review in any future partial or final award, and should be distinguished from a partial award (*see 8.04*).

7.35   This power should be used with care. For example, if a payment is ordered the respondent may become bankrupt and be unable to continue with its defence, a situation which could result in substantial injustice being done, particularly if it later transpires that the payment ordered provisionally is higher than the final award. It may be useful in situations where it is clear that there is some liability, for example where a breach of contract has been admitted but the amount of damages only is in dispute, but even here it should be used with caution.

Multi-party arbitrations

7.36   Unless the parties agree, the arbitrator has no power to order consolidation of proceedings or concurrent hearings (S.35). A consolidation of proceedings is the combining of different but related claims into a single proceeding, whereas in concurrent hearings the claims remain separate, but are heard together for the sake of convenience and the saving of costs.

7.37   In construction disputes there are frequently more than two parties with a direct involvement in a matter under dispute, and one party may wish to bring a third or fourth party into an arbitration. From the point of view of the employer, where there is a dispute about whether a default was caused by the main contractor or a nominated subcontractor, the employer may wish to bring actions against them both. The main contractor may wish to bring in a subcontractor when a claim is made by the employer which the main contractor considers is the subcontractor's fault. The subcontractor is less likely to wish to bring the employer into any proceedings against the main contractor, except possibly if the subcontractor's right to payment depends on the contractor having received payment.

7.38   In all these examples, although it may be in the interests of one party to bring in a third party, it is unlikely that the second will gain any benefit from having the third brought in. In fact the contrary is more likely: the presence of a third party will prolong the proceedings and increase the expense. It is unlikely that agreement will be reached between all the parties once the dispute has arisen, and it is therefore important to agree in advance the circumstances under which parties are prepared to be brought into another arbitration.

7.39   The JCT standard forms generally provide for multi-party proceedings between employer, main contractor and nominated subcontractors. The clauses, often called 'back to back' provisions, seek to equate procedures with High Court procedures for the resolution of multi-party disputes. Clause 41.2.1 of JCT 80 (of which there is a matching clause in NSC/C) states:

'Provided that if the dispute or difference to be referred to arbitration under this Contract raises issues which are substantially the same as or connected with issues raised in a related dispute between:
the Employer and Nominated Sub-Contractor under Agreement NSC/W, *or*

the Contractor and any Nominated Sub-Contractor under a
Nominated Sub-Contract, *or*
the Contractor and/or the Employer and any Nominated Supplier
whose contract of sale with the Contractor provides for the matters
referred to in clause 36.4.8.2
and if the related dispute has already been referred for determination
to a Arbitrator, the Employer and the Contractor hereby agree
that the dispute or difference under this Contract shall be referred to
the Arbitrator appointed to determine the related dispute ... (and),
that such Arbitrator shall have power to make such directions and all
necessary awards in the same way as if the procedure of the High
Court as to joining one or more defendants or joining co-defendants
or third parties was available to the parties and to him.'

7.40   The JCT clauses effectively bind the parties; the Employer and
Contractor have agreed in advance that a third party may be enjoined
in their arbitration, and that their dispute may be heard by an
arbitrator in another arbitration (*Trafalgar House Construction
(Regions) Ltd v Railtrack plc*, 1995). However multi-party
arbitrations give rise to various complex questions, not all of which
are expressly answered by the JCT 'back to back' clauses.

7.41   For example, the clauses require that the disputes should have subject
matter in common, but do not specify how the degree of commonality
is to be determined and by whom. As discussed under 5.24, under
Section 30 the arbitrator can rule on questions regarding his or her
own jurisdiction, unless the parties have made an agreement to the
contrary. Therefore an arbitrator already appointed could rule on
whether the subject matter of a related dispute, raised by one of the
parties, was sufficiently in common to satisfy the requirements of the
back to back clauses. However if the parties have excluded this power,
and if they cannot agree on the matter it would need to be determined
by the court (*Hyundai Engineering and Construction Co Ltd v Active
Building and Civil Construction Ltd*, 1988).

7.42   The timing is also critical. Where a subcontract dispute is to be joined
to a dispute under the main contract, under the JCT clauses the
decision has to be made after a dispute has arisen on the subcontract,
and after an arbitrator has been appointed to hear a related dispute
on the main contract (*Trafalgar House v Railtrack*) but before an
arbitrator has been appointed on the subcontract dispute. Once
validly appointed that appointment cannot normally be revoked
(*Higgs & Hill Building Ltd v Campbell Denis Ltd and Another*, 1982).

Only if the arbitrator is appointed on the subcontract dispute after the main contractor has validly invoked the proviso requiring the subcontract dispute to be joined to one under the main contract, will that arbitrator have no jurisdiction (*M J Gleeson Group plc v Wyatt of Snetterton Ltd*, 1994).

7.43   There is also the question of how the disputes are to be joined, ie are the disputes to be heard concurrently or consolidated, and if the latter who will be the claimants or co-claimants and who the respondents or co-respondents. This is something which JCT 80 empowers the arbitrator to do (*see 7.39*), and which he or she must determine and give specific directions on (*Trafalgar House v Railtrack*).

8   The award

8.01   As with other aspects of arbitration, the parties are free to agree matters concerning the award, which can take a very wide variety of forms. In essence it should set out the decision reached on every question referred to the arbitrator and, unless otherwise agreed by the parties, the reasons for reaching those decisions, including relevant findings of fact. The arbitrator must decide the issues according to the law, unless the parties have agreed some other basis (S.46), eg that the arbitrator could decide according to general principles of justness and fairness. (This is unlikely to happen except in international arbitration.) In order for it to be complete the award should also deal with allocation of costs. Various aspects of the award are discussed in more detail below.

Timing

8.02   If the time is limited in the agreement, and for some reason the arbitrator fails to make an award within the prescribed time, then the arbitrator may lose the right to make an award later and any award will be void. A first course of action is for the arbitrator to apply to the parties requesting they agree an amendment to the arbitration agreement allowing the arbitrator to make a later award. However one party may refuse to agree and in this event, unless the parties have agreed otherwise, the court may extend the time for making an award on application by the arbitrator or one of the parties, if it is satisfied that otherwise a substantial injustice would be done (S.50).

8.03   With some procedural rules, in particular the International Chamber of Commerce rules, extensions may be made by the institution, so it is to the institution that the application must be made in the first instance. It would be extremely unlikely for the court to reverse the decision of an institution.

Awards on different issues

8.04   Unless otherwise agreed by the parties the arbitrator may make more than one award on different issues. These used to be referred to as 'interim awards', and are now frequently termed 'partial awards' although the Act uses neither of these terms (*Rutherford and Sims*, 1997). The award could relate to an issue affecting the whole of the claim, or to a part of the claim (S.47). Any such award is not temporary or of a provisional nature (*see 7.34*) but final with respect to the matters with which it deals.

8.05   This is a useful power which may be used to determine at an early stage some question which is of central or fundamental significance, and the answer to which could remove the necessity to consider many related questions. For example, one party may be claiming that certain information was provided late, that this caused a delay which entitled the contractor to an extension of time of a certain number of weeks, and which had also resulted in an unjustified deduction of liquidated damages. If the arbitrator can make an early award which states that the information was provided on time, much time and effort can be saved in arguing the related questions.

8.06   The making of an award regarding one fundamental question may sometimes even result in the parties being able settle all the outstanding matters without continuing with the arbitration. An award regarding the substantive matters may also be used to allow for the parties to address the arbitrator on the matters of costs (*see 8.11*).

Settlement

8.07   If the dispute is settled during the proceedings (*see 7.21*) then the arbitrator may issue an agreed award recording the settlement, if requested to do so by the parties (S.51(2)). Unless the parties have settled the question of costs, the arbitrator may also make an award as to costs according to the provisions of the Act. An award recording the settlement has the same effect as any other award, and would be capable of being enforced as a judgment of the court. It is therefore a strong argument for entering into an arbitration process, even where there is a good chance of settlement at an early stage, as the parties will be compelled to stand by the decision reached to a degree which cannot be achieved by any other dispute resolution process.

Remedies

8.08   Section 48 of the Act gives the parties the right to agree on the remedies available to the arbitrator. This is a discretion even wider than that exercisable by a court. For example, they could give the arbitrator the power to award punitive damages, or to make an order for specific performance in circumstances where the court would be

unable to do so. If the parties have not agreed otherwise, the
arbitrator has the power to do all of the following (S.48):

· *Order the payment of a sum of money*
  The most common form of award.
· *Make a declaration on any matter to be determined*
  A declaration is the determination of the rights between the parties.
  For example, the arbitrator may make a decision as to whether a
  term should be implied into a contract, or as to the meaning of a
  particular clause.
· *Order a party to do or refrain from doing something*
  It is unlikely that an arbitrator would make an award of this sort,
  often termed an 'injunction', due to the lack of ancillary powers of
  enforcement.
· *Order specific performance*
· *Order the rectification, setting aside or cancellation of a deed or any
  document*
  The arbitrator may order, for example, that a contract may be
  corrected so that it reflects the true agreement between the parties.

In spite of the wide reaching powers conferred by the Act, an award
in a construction arbitration will almost always be for a sum of
money unless there are very special circumstances which suggest that
some alternative direction would be more appropriate.

Interest

8.09   Section 49 of the Act provides that the arbitrator may, unless
         otherwise agreed by the parties, award simple or compound interest:
         · on the whole or part of any amount awarded up to the date of the
           award;
         · on the whole or part of any payment made up to the date of
           payment;
         · on the amount of the award from the date of the award or later.

8.10   The power to award compound interest has provoked much surprise
         and comment, as this power is not available to the courts except in
         exceptional circumstances. In the first two of the above circumstances,
         the arbitrator will normally award interest from the date at which that
         sum should have been paid. For example, where a contractor has
         refused to allow a sum to the employer in liquidated damages,
         contending that an extension of time should have been awarded, and
         the arbitrator determines that the liquidated damages were deductible,

then interest may be awarded from the date that the sum should have been paid to the employer up to the date of the award. The arbitrator should always make an award as to interest to be payable on the amount in the award from the date by which the amount is to be paid.

Costs

8.11   The costs incurred during an arbitration can often exceed the amount originally claimed, therefore determining who shall pay these costs is a matter of some importance. The arbitrator has the power to award costs, and must do so unless the parties agree otherwise (S.61(1–2)). Any agreement that a party will pay the whole or part of its costs in any event is not valid unless entered into after the dispute has arisen (S.60). Any agreement as to allocation of costs is only applied to such costs as are recoverable (*see 8.15*). By 'costs' is meant the arbitrator's fees and expenses, which can include the costs of advisors and assessors; the parties' costs, including any legal costs, any fees etc charged by any appointing institution; and costs incurred in determining the amount of recoverable costs (S.59).

8.12   Unless the parties have agreed some other basis, the Act states that the costs should be awarded on the basis that the loser pays all the recoverable costs, unless the arbitrator feels that this would be inappropriate (S.61(2)). This would be the practice in court proceedings, and was generally the practice in arbitration prior to the Act. The arbitrator therefore has a discretion not to follow this rule in all cases, but should nevertheless not depart from it without good reason, and arbitrators' awards have on occasion been set aside or remitted where the arbitrator has failed to exercise this discretion judicially (*Metro-Cammell Hong Kong Ltd v FKI Engineering plc*, 1996). Such a failure might under the Act be an error of law on which an appeal could be brought.

8.13   Circumstances where it may be appropriate are where a party has conducted itself during the arbitration in a way that has resulted in unnecessary delay and expense. After an interlocutory hearing, for example, the arbitrator may order that certain costs will be borne by the claimant 'in any event', ie whether the claimant wins or loses, and this order would be picked up in the final award. Another circumstance might be where a party had misconducted itself in relation to the contract out of which the arbitration has arisen.

8.14 Where a claimant only recovers part of what is claimed, the whole of the costs are still normally awarded. However, if a great deal of time is spent on several heads of claim which in some way were spurious, the arbitrator may award these costs to the respondent. Where there has been an offer which has not been taken up, this will also usually affect the awarding of costs (*see 7.21*). The costs of a counterclaim are generally awarded on the same basis as the claim – in other words, the winner in the counterclaim will be awarded its costs.

8.15 Generally parties to court actions and arbitrations do not recover all their costs. The fact that a winning party has been awarded its costs will not necessarily mean that the winner will receive all those costs. Unless the parties agree otherwise, only 'recoverable' costs will be awarded, however they are to be apportioned between the parties. This practice developed to avoid the problem of a party being able to engage the most expensive of advisors and generally to squander time and money, and nevertheless get these costs refunded, even where the opposing party had been more reasonable. Under Section 63 the parties are free to agree which costs are recoverable; if they do not, the arbitrator or the court may determine the recoverable costs on such basis as it thinks fit. In practice, agreement is commonly reached, but sometimes the process breaks down. The process of determining which costs are recoverable is frequently referred to as 'taxing', though the Act does not use this term.

8.16 There are several bases commonly used for calculating recoverable costs. The one set out in the Act, 'a reasonable amount in respect of all costs reasonably incurred, (with) any doubt … resolved in favour of the paying party' (S.63(5)), is equivalent to the 'standard basis' currently used in court. Alternatives to this are the 'indemnity basis' where the receiving party is awarded all costs except any unreasonable amount, or costs unreasonably incurred, with any payment in doubt being resolved in favour of the recipient. This is clearly much more onerous and would rarely be used by an arbitrator except where the paying party had deliberately caused unnecessary costs, and only when a party has applied for an order on this basis. It is now increasingly common for arbitrators to award costs on a 'commercial basis'. The parties submit accounts of costs actually incurred, rather than the solicitors' bills of costs normally presented for taxation. Whichever basis is used, the arbitrator should set this out in the award for the benefit of the parties.

8.17   With respect to the arbitrator's own fees and expenses, the Act states that only such reasonable fees and expenses as are appropriate in the circumstances are recoverable (S.64(1)). This is to do with recoverability as between the parties, and does not affect any contractual right of the arbitrator to payment (S.64(4)). Where the parties cannot agree on the recoverable costs, they must apply to the court to determine the arbitrator's fees and expenses (S.64(2)).

Power to limit recoverable costs

8.18   Section 65 of the Act gives the arbitrator, unless the parties agree otherwise, the power to limit the recoverable costs to a specific amount. This limit would operate irrespective of who will bear the eventual costs. The limit can be imposed on the whole costs, but could also be imposed on only a section of the costs, for example with respect to a specific claim, a particular event (eg discovery) or even costs incurred during a particular period of time.

8.19   This is a new power, and one to be exercised with care. It does not, of course, limit what parties may actually spend, only what they can hope to recover from the other party. The limitation can be placed at any time, but the parties must be given sufficient notice to allow them to take it into account. Therefore though the parties will not know how costs will be capped on entering into the arbitration, unless they have limited it by agreement, they will know in reasonable advance of incurring the costs themselves. The arguments regarding the merits of capping recoverable costs are complex, and closely related to those for or against provisions for parties bearing all their own costs.

8.20   The aim of a limitation is to curb unnecessary and extravagant spending, and encourage parties to take a sensible view of their dispute. Even if a party wins, that party will still have expended money which is irrecoverable, and at a certain point this will begin to seem out of proportion to the sum at stake. At any rate it will become pointless to pursue the argument simply in order to avoid losing costs, as these will be lost whatever the outcome. For example, if the sum in dispute is £50,000, and the arbitrator limits the costs recoverable to a global figure of £10,000, the maximum either party can hope to win is £60,000. With this figure at the back of their minds they may be more inclined to accept an offer of say £40,000 than if, as before, they could continue the argument indefinitely in the belief that they stood to win £50,000 plus most of what they spent.

8.21   When there is a limitation on costs, a poorer party may be able to continue with an arbitration without risking having to pay for the extravagant tastes of its opponent, assuming the arbitrator limits the costs to as least as much as the amount the arbitrator anticipates the poorer party will expend. In this way it prevents a financially stronger party forcing a weaker one to compromise by using the threat of excessive costs. However if the limit is set too low, it may disadvantage a party who genuinely has a more expensive case to bring. It would almost certainly be inappropriate to limit costs in major contracts between equally balanced parties, where the amounts at stake may appear to them to justify limitless expenditure. If the arbitrator does place a limit on costs, this should be reviewed as the arbitration progresses.

Form of the award

8.22   For the first time in English law formal requirements are set out for the form of an award. Unless otherwise agreed the award is to be in writing, signed by the arbitrator, contain reasons (unless an agreed award, *see 8.07*) and state the date and seat of the award (S.52). The requirement for reasons represents a significant change from the law prior to the Act, when reasons were only necessary if specifically requested. Parties should appreciate that if they agree not to require reasons in the award, then this will effectively eliminate a possible appeal on a point of law. Sections 52, 53 and 54 of the Act state what happens if no date or seat is given.

Notification and arbitrator's lien

8.23   The arbitrator must notify the parties without delay once the award has been made (S.55). The arbitrator has the right to refuse to deliver the award except on full payment of his or her fees and expenses (S.56(1)). This section of the Act is mandatory and cannot be excluded by agreement. Normally one of the parties will take up the award by paying the arbitrator's fees, and the costs will be settled between them as set out in the award, or that party may apply later to the court to make an adjustment under Section 28. The arbitrator usually sends a copy of the award to the other party once it has been taken up.

8.24   As an alternative, if a party feels that the arbitrator's fee is too high, it may apply to the court to have the award delivered into court, upon payment into court of either the full fee or a reduced fee set by the court (S.56(2–4)). The court can then tax the arbitrator's fees, and any balance will be returned to the applicant.

Power to correct

8.25   Unless otherwise agreed, the arbitrator may correct an award or make an additional award on application of one of the parties or on his or her own initiative within 28 days, or later if the parties agree (S.57). The power to correct is limited to clerical mistakes or slips, and to remove any ambiguity. The power to make an additional award covers claims referred to the arbitrator but not dealt with in the award. The arbitrator must allow the parties reasonable opportunity to make representations regarding corrections.

Effect of the award

8.26   An award is final and binding on the parties, unless otherwise agreed (S.58). Neither party may re-open any matter decided in the award by any form of proceedings, except for challenges as provided for in the Act. The parties may agree that the award should have a different effect. This imports a degree of flexibility into the arbitration proceedings. For example, a short form arbitration could result in an award agreed to be temporarily binding until resolution in a subsequent arbitration following practical completion of the contract.

Enforcement

8.27   Any award may, by leave of the court, be enforced in the same manner as a judgment of the court (S.66). This section of the Act may not be excluded by agreement. Court procedures available for the enforcement of the award include, if the award is for a sum of money, the seizure and sale of the respondent's goods, the interception of a debt due to the respondent, and the charging and sale of the respondent's property. Where the award is in the form of an injunction the court's powers include imprisonment. The court's enforcement is discretionary. The circumstances under which it may refuse to enforce an award would generally be governed by common law rules, and would include such matters as the award being defective, or deciding matters not capable of resolution by arbitration. The court may not enforce an award where the person against whom it is to be enforced can show that the arbitrator lacked jurisdiction to make the award (S.66(3)).

Challenging the award

8.28 Any party may challenge the award in court on the grounds of lack of substantive jurisdiction (S.67). This is a new, mandatory section, and is subject to the following restrictions:
- any available arbitral process must have been exhausted (S.70(2)(a));
- any relevant application to correct an award has been made under Section 57 (S.70(2)(b));
- the application is brought within 28 days of the date of the award (S.70(3)), subject to the court's power to extend time under Section 80(5). This is an increase in time from the old legislation where the limit was 21 days;
- the right must not have been lost due to delay (S.73).

The court may confirm the award, vary it or set it aside in whole or in part.

8.29 A party may also challenge the award on the grounds of serious irregularity, subject to Section 70 and 73 restrictions as above. A definitive list of what may constitute serious irregularity is set out in Section 68(2)(a), including failure to comply with Section 33, the general obligations of the arbitrator, and the arbitrator exceeding his or her powers. Failure to comply with the arbitrator's general duties is clearly a broad concept, and it will be left to case law to determine the boundaries of serious irregularity. The irregularity must have caused or will cause, substantial injustice to the applicant. If an irregularity is shown the court may remit the award to the arbitrator, set it aside or declare it of no effect, either in whole or in part (S.68). Remission should be the normal course, unless it is inappropriate, as the other alternatives will place the parties back at the position they were at the start of the arbitration. In practice, remission is likely to be the normal remedy.

Appeal procedures

8.30   An appeal may be brought on a point of law under Section 69 of the
        Act if either all the parties agree, or by leave of the court. The parties
        can by agreement exclude the right of appeal. This agreement can be
        made before or after the commencement of the arbitration (the
        Section 87 requirements for domestic arbitrations were not brought
        into force), but it should be made in writing. JCT forms contain a
        term giving consent to an appeal in advance, which has been upheld
        as valid (*Vascroft (Contractors) Ltd v Seeboard plc*, 1996).

8.31   There are many restrictions on the nature of issues that can be
        appealed. Generally finality is upheld, but the parties are assumed not
        to have agreed to accept a decision that is clearly wrong in law. The
        court may only grant leave if it believes that:
        · determination of the question will substantially affect the rights of
          one of the parties; and
        · the question is one the arbitrator was asked to decide; and
        · on the facts found in the award the question is obviously wrongly
          decided, or one of public importance; and
        · it is just and proper for the court to do so (S.69(3)).

8.32   The appeal must be brought within 28 days of the award, and any
        available arbitral process must have been exhausted. The court may
        confirm or vary the award, remit the award to the arbitrator, or set it
        aside either in whole or in part. Remission should be the normal
        course, unless this is inappropriate. Normally a hearing will not be
        required, thus avoiding argument, time and expense, and the court
        will decide the matter on documents alone. The scope for a further
        appeal to the Court of Appeal is very limited.

References

Cases

Aughton Ltd v M F Kent Services Ltd
[1991] 57 BLR 1

Cape Durasteel Ltd v Rosser and Russell Building Services Ltd
[1995] 46 Con LR 75

Cruden Construction Ltd v Commission for the New Towns
[1994] 75 BLR 134

Higgs & Hill Building Ltd v Campbell Denis Ltd and Another
[1982] 28 BLR 47

*Hyundai Engineering and Construction Co Ltd v Active Building and Civil
Construction PteE Ltd*
[1988] 45 BLR 62

M J Gleeson Group plc v Wyatt of Snetterton Ltd
[1994] 72 BLR 15

Metro-Cammell Hong Kong Ltd v FKI Engineering plc
[1996] 77 BLR 84

Monmouthshire County Council v Costelloe & Kemple
[1965] 5 BLR 83

Northern Regional Health Authority v Derek Crouch Construction Company
[1984] QB 644, 26 BLR 1

Tarmac Construction Limited v Esso Petroleum Limited
[1996] 51 CLR 187

Trafalgar House Construction (Regions) Ltd v Railtrack plc
[1995] 75 BLR 55

University of Reading v Miller Construction Ltd and David Sharp
[1994] 75 BLR 91

Vascroft (Contractors) Ltd v Seeboard plc
[1996] 78 BLR 132

Publications

Cornes, D. (1996)
'The Second Edition of the New Engineering Contract'.
International Construction Law Review 13 (January): 96–119

Cornes, D (1994)
Design Liability in the Construction Industry
Oxford, Blackwells Scientific Publications

Harris, B., Planterose, R. et al. (1996)
The Arbitration Act 1966: A Commentary
Oxford, Blackwell Science Ltd

JCT (1997)
Note to Users: Arbitration
London, RIBA Publications.

Mustill, S. M. and Boyd, S. (1989)
Commercial Arbitration
London, Butterworths

Rutherford, M. and Sims, J. (1996)
Arbitration Act 1996: A Practical Guide
London, FT Law & Tax

Wallace, I. D. (1997a)
'First Impressions of the 1996 Arbitration Act.'
The International Construction Law Review 14 (January): 71–97

Wallace, I. D. (1997b)
'Another Loose Cannon in the Court of Appeal: Not What the Parties Meant and the Shadow of Crouch.'
Construction Law Journal 13(1): 3–20

Arbitration Act 1996

The Act received the Royal Assent on 17 June 1996 and, apart from Sections 85–87, came into force on 31 January 1997.

Appendix A contains the full text of the Act as published by HMSO, with the exception of the Schedules.

Arbitration Act 1996

CHAPTER 23

ARRANGEMENT OF SECTIONS

Part I

Arbitration pursuant to an arbitration agreement

Introductory

PART II

OTHER PROVISIONS RELATING TO ARBITRATION

Domestic arbitration agreements

Consumer arbitration agreements

Small claims arbitration in the county court

Arbitration Act 1996

1996 CHAPTER 23

An Act to restate and improve the law relating to arbitration pursuant to an arbitration agreement; to make other provision relating to arbitration and arbitration awards; and for connected purposes.   [17th June 1996]

BE IT ENACTED by the Queen's most Excellent Majesty, by and with the advice and consent of the Lords Spiritual and Temporal, and Commons, in this present Parliament assembled, and by the authority of the same, as follows:—

PART I

ARBITRATION PURSUANT TO AN ARBITRATION AGREEMENT

Introductory

1. The provisions of this Part are founded on the following principles, and shall be construed accordingly— General principles.

    (a) the object of arbitration is to obtain the fair resolution of disputes by an impartial tribunal without unnecessary delay or expense;

    (b) the parties should be free to agree how their disputes are resolved, subject only to such safeguards as are necessary in the public interest;

    (c) in matters governed by this Part the court should not intervene except as provided by this Part.

2.—(1) The provisions of this Part apply where the seat of the arbitration is in England and Wales or Northern Ireland. Scope of application of provisions.

    (2) The following sections apply even if the seat of the arbitration is outside England and Wales or Northern Ireland or no seat has been designated or determined—

    (a) sections 9 to 11 (stay of legal proceedings, &c.), and

    (b) section 66 (enforcement of arbitral awards).

(3) The powers conferred by the following sections apply even if the seat of the arbitration is outside England and Wales or Northern Ireland or no seat has been designated or determined—

   (a) section 43 (securing the attendance of witnesses), and

   (b) section 44 (court powers exercisable in support of arbitral proceedings);

but the court may refuse to exercise any such power if, in the opinion of the court, the fact that the seat of the arbitration is outside England and Wales or Northern Ireland, or that when designated or determined the seat is likely to be outside England and Wales or Northern Ireland, makes it inappropriate to do so.

(4) The court may exercise a power conferred by any provision of this Part not mentioned in subsection (2) or (3) for the purpose of supporting the arbitral process where—

   (a) no seat of the arbitration has been designated or determined, and

   (b) by reason of a connection with England and Wales or Northern Ireland the court is satisfied that it is appropriate to do so.

(5) Section 7 (separability of arbitration agreement) and section 8 (death of a party) apply where the law applicable to the arbitration agreement is the law of England and Wales or Northern Ireland even if the seat of the arbitration is outside England and Wales or Northern Ireland or has not been designated or determined.

The seat of the arbitration.

3. In this Part "the seat of the arbitration" means the juridical seat of the arbitration designated—

   (a) by the parties to the arbitration agreement, or

   (b) by any arbitral or other institution or person vested by the parties with powers in that regard, or

   (c) by the arbitral tribunal if so authorised by the parties,

or determined, in the absence of any such designation, having regard to the parties' agreement and all the relevant circumstances.

Mandatory and non-mandatory provisions.

4.—(1) The mandatory provisions of this Part are listed in Schedule 1 and have effect notwithstanding any agreement to the contrary.

(2) The other provisions of this Part (the "non-mandatory provisions") allow the parties to make their own arrangements by agreement but provide rules which apply in the absence of such agreement.

(3) The parties may make such arrangements by agreeing to the application of institutional rules or providing any other means by which a matter may be decided.

(4) It is immaterial whether or not the law applicable to the parties' agreement is the law of England and Wales or, as the case may be, Northern Ireland.

(5) The choice of a law other than the law of England and Wales or Northern Ireland as the applicable law in respect of a matter provided for by a non-mandatory provision of this Part is equivalent to an agreement making provision about that matter.

For this purpose an applicable law determined in accordance with the parties' agreement, or which is objectively determined in the absence of any express or implied choice, shall be treated as chosen by the parties.

5.—(1) The provisions of this Part apply only where the arbitration agreement is in writing, and any other agreement between the parties as to any matter is effective for the purposes of this Part only if in writing.

Agreements to be in writing.

The expressions "agreement", "agree" and "agreed" shall be construed accordingly.

(2) There is an agreement in writing—

(a) if the agreement is made in writing (whether or not it is signed by the parties),

(b) if the agreement is made by exchange of communications in writing, or

(c) if the agreement is evidenced in writing.

(3) Where parties agree otherwise than in writing by reference to terms which are in writing, they make an agreement in writing.

(4) An agreement is evidenced in writing if an agreement made otherwise than in writing is recorded by one of the parties, or by a third party, with the authority of the parties to the agreement.

(5) An exchange of written submissions in arbitral or legal proceedings in which the existence of an agreement otherwise than in writing is alleged by one party against another party and not denied by the other party in his response constitutes as between those parties an agreement in writing to the effect alleged.

(6) References in this Part to anything being written or in writing include its being recorded by any means.

The arbitration agreement

6.—(1) In this Part an "arbitration agreement" means an agreement to submit to arbitration present or future disputes (whether they are contractual or not).

Definition of arbitration agreement.

(2) The reference in an agreement to a written form of arbitration clause or to a document containing an arbitration clause constitutes an arbitration agreement if the reference is such as to make that clause part of the agreement.

7. Unless otherwise agreed by the parties, an arbitration agreement which forms or was intended to form part of another agreement (whether or not in writing) shall not be regarded as invalid, non-existent or ineffective because that other agreement is invalid, or did not come into existence or has become ineffective, and it shall for that purpose be treated as a distinct agreement.

Separability of arbitration agreement.

8.—(1) Unless otherwise agreed by the parties, an arbitration agreement is not discharged by the death of a party and may be enforced by or against the personal representatives of that party.

Whether agreement discharged by death of a party.

(2) Subsection (1) does not affect the operation of any enactment or rule of law by virtue of which a substantive right or obligation is extinguished by death.

Stay of legal proceedings

Stay of legal proceedings.

9.—(1) A party to an arbitration agreement against whom legal proceedings are brought (whether by way of claim or counterclaim) in respect of a matter which under the agreement is to be referred to arbitration may (upon notice to the other parties to the proceedings) apply to the court in which the proceedings have been brought to stay the proceedings so far as they concern that matter.

(2) An application may be made notwithstanding that the matter is to be referred to arbitration only after the exhaustion of other dispute resolution procedures.

(3) An application may not be made by a person before taking the appropriate procedural step (if any) to acknowledge the legal proceedings against him or after he has taken any step in those proceedings to answer the substantive claim.

(4) On an application under this section the court shall grant a stay unless satisfied that the arbitration agreement is null and void, inoperative, or incapable of being performed.

(5) If the court refuses to stay the legal proceedings, any provision that an award is a condition precedent to the bringing of legal proceedings in respect of any matter is of no effect in relation to those proceedings.

Reference of interpleader issue to arbitration.

10.—(1) Where in legal proceedings relief by way of interpleader is granted and any issue between the claimants is one in respect of which there is an arbitration agreement between them, the court granting the relief shall direct that the issue be determined in accordance with the agreement unless the circumstances are such that proceedings brought by a claimant in respect of the matter would not be stayed.

(2) Where subsection (1) applies but the court does not direct that the issue be determined in accordance with the arbitration agreement, any provision that an award is a condition precedent to the bringing of legal proceedings in respect of any matter shall not affect the determination of that issue by the court.

Retention of security where Admiralty proceedings stayed.

11.—(1) Where Admiralty proceedings are stayed on the ground that the dispute in question should be submitted to arbitration, the court granting the stay may, if in those proceedings property has been arrested or bail or other security has been given to prevent or obtain release from arrest—

    (a) order that the property arrested be retained as security for the satisfaction of any award given in the arbitration in respect of that dispute, or

    (b) order that the stay of those proceedings be conditional on the provision of equivalent security for the satisfaction of any such award.

(2) Subject to any provision made by rules of court and to any necessary modifications, the same law and practice shall apply in relation to property retained in pursuance of an order as would apply if it were held for the purposes of proceedings in the court making the order.

Commencement of arbitral proceedings

12.—(1) Where an arbitration agreement to refer future disputes to arbitration provides that a claim shall be barred, or the claimant's right extinguished, unless the claimant takes within a time fixed by the agreement some step—

    (a) to begin arbitral proceedings, or

    (b) to begin other dispute resolution procedures which must be exhausted before arbitral proceedings can be begun,

the court may by order extend the time for taking that step.

Power of court to extend time for beginning arbitral proceedings, &c.

(2) Any party to the arbitration agreement may apply for such an order (upon notice to the other parties), but only after a claim has arisen and after exhausting any available arbitral process for obtaining an extension of time.

(3) The court shall make an order only if satisfied—

    (a) that the circumstances are such as were outside the reasonable contemplation of the parties when they agreed the provision in question, and that it would be just to extend the time, or

    (b) that the conduct of one party makes it unjust to hold the other party to the strict terms of the provision in question.

(4) The court may extend the time for such period and on such terms as it thinks fit, and may do so whether or not the time previously fixed (by agreement or by a previous order) has expired.

(5) An order under this section does not affect the operation of the Limitation Acts (see section 13).

(6) The leave of the court is required for any appeal from a decision of the court under this section.

13.—(1) The Limitation Acts apply to arbitral proceedings as they apply to legal proceedings.

Application of Limitation Acts.

(2) The court may order that in computing the time prescribed by the Limitation Acts for the commencement of proceedings (including arbitral proceedings) in respect of a dispute which was the subject matter—

    (a) of an award which the court orders to be set aside or declares to be of no effect, or

    (b) of the affected part of an award which the court orders to be set aside in part, or declares to be in part of no effect,

the period between the commencement of the arbitration and the date of the order referred to in paragraph (a) or (b) shall be excluded.

(3) In determining for the purposes of the Limitation Acts when a cause of action accrued, any provision that an award is a condition precedent to the bringing of legal proceedings in respect of a matter to which an arbitration agreement applies shall be disregarded.

(4) In this Part "the Limitation Acts" means—

    (a) in England and Wales, the Limitation Act 1980, the Foreign Limitation Periods Act 1984 and any other enactment (whenever passed) relating to the limitation of actions;

1980 c. 58.
1984 c. 16.

PART I
S.I. 1989/1339
(N.I. 11).
S.I. 1985/754 (N.I.
5).

(b) in Northern Ireland, the Limitation (Northern Ireland) Order 1989, the Foreign Limitation Periods (Northern Ireland) Order 1985 and any other enactment (whenever passed) relating to the limitation of actions.

Commencement of arbitral proceedings.

14.—(1) The parties are free to agree when arbitral proceedings are to be regarded as commenced for the purposes of this Part and for the purposes of the Limitation Acts.

(2) If there is no such agreement the following provisions apply.

(3) Where the arbitrator is named or designated in the arbitration agreement, arbitral proceedings are commenced in respect of a matter when one party serves on the other party or parties a notice in writing requiring him or them to submit that matter to the person so named or designated.

(4) Where the arbitrator or arbitrators are to be appointed by the parties, arbitral proceedings are commenced in respect of a matter when one party serves on the other party or parties notice in writing requiring him or them to appoint an arbitrator or to agree to the appointment of an arbitrator in respect of that matter.

(5) Where the arbitrator or arbitrators are to be appointed by a person other than a party to the proceedings, arbitral proceedings are commenced in respect of a matter when one party gives notice in writing to that person requesting him to make the appointment in respect of that matter.

The arbitral tribunal

The arbitral tribunal.

15.—(1) The parties are free to agree on the number of arbitrators to form the tribunal and whether there is to be a chairman or umpire.

(2) Unless otherwise agreed by the parties, an agreement that the number of arbitrators shall be two or any other even number shall be understood as requiring the appointment of an additional arbitrator as chairman of the tribunal.

(3) If there is no agreement as to the number of arbitrators, the tribunal shall consist of a sole arbitrator.

Procedure for appointment of arbitrators.

16.—(1) The parties are free to agree on the procedure for appointing the arbitrator or arbitrators, including the procedure for appointing any chairman or umpire.

(2) If or to the extent that there is no such agreement, the following provisions apply.

(3) If the tribunal is to consist of a sole arbitrator, the parties shall jointly appoint the arbitrator not later than 28 days after service of a request in writing by either party to do so.

(4) If the tribunal is to consist of two arbitrators, each party shall appoint one arbitrator not later than 14 days after service of a request in writing by either party to do so.

(5) If the tribunal is to consist of three arbitrators—

(a) each party shall appoint one arbitrator not later than 14 days after service of a request in writing by either party to do so, and

    (b) the two so appointed shall forthwith appoint a third arbitrator as the chairman of the tribunal.

(6) If the tribunal is to consist of two arbitrators and an umpire—

    (a) each party shall appoint one arbitrator not later than 14 days after service of a request in writing by either party to do so, and

    (b) the two so appointed may appoint an umpire at any time after they themselves are appointed and shall do so before any substantive hearing or forthwith if they cannot agree on a matter relating to the arbitration.

(7) In any other case (in particular, if there are more than two parties) section 18 applies as in the case of a failure of the agreed appointment procedure.

17.—(1) Unless the parties otherwise agree, where each of two parties to an arbitration agreement is to appoint an arbitrator and one party ("the party in default") refuses to do so, or fails to do so within the time specified, the other party, having duly appointed his arbitrator, may give notice in writing to the party in default that he proposes to appoint his arbitrator to act as sole arbitrator.
Power in case of default to appoint sole arbitrator.

(2) If the party in default does not within 7 clear days of that notice being given—

    (a) make the required appointment, and

    (b) notify the other party that he has done so,

the other party may appoint his arbitrator as sole arbitrator whose award shall be binding on both parties as if he had been so appointed by agreement.

(3) Where a sole arbitrator has been appointed under subsection (2), the party in default may (upon notice to the appointing party) apply to the court which may set aside the appointment.

(4) The leave of the court is required for any appeal from a decision of the court under this section.

18.—(1) The parties are free to agree what is to happen in the event of a failure of the procedure for the appointment of the arbitral tribunal.
Failure of appointment procedure.

    There is no failure if an appointment is duly made under section 17 (power in case of default to appoint sole arbitrator), unless that appointment is set aside.

(2) If or to the extent that there is no such agreement any party to the arbitration agreement may (upon notice to the other parties) apply to the court to exercise its powers under this section.

(3) Those powers are—

    (a) to give directions as to the making of any necessary appointments;

    (b) to direct that the tribunal shall be constituted by such appointments (or any one or more of them) as have been made;

    (c) to revoke any appointments already made;

    (d) to make any necessary appointments itself.

(4) An appointment made by the court under this section has effect as if made with the agreement of the parties.

(5) The leave of the court is required for any appeal from a decision of the court under this section.

Court to have regard to agreed qualifications.

19. In deciding whether to exercise, and in considering how to exercise, any of its powers under section 16 (procedure for appointment of arbitrators) or section 18 (failure of appointment procedure), the court shall have due regard to any agreement of the parties as to the qualifications required of the arbitrators.

Chairman.

20.—(1) Where the parties have agreed that there is to be a chairman, they are free to agree what the functions of the chairman are to be in relation to the making of decisions, orders and awards.

(2) If or to the extent that there is no such agreement, the following provisions apply.

(3) Decisions, orders and awards shall be made by all or a majority of the arbitrators (including the chairman).

(4) The view of the chairman shall prevail in relation to a decision, order or award in respect of which there is neither unanimity nor a majority under subsection (3).

Umpire.

21.—(1) Where the parties have agreed that there is to be an umpire, they are free to agree what the functions of the umpire are to be, and in particular—

(a) whether he is to attend the proceedings, and

(b) when he is to replace the other arbitrators as the tribunal with power to make decisions, orders and awards.

(2) If or to the extent that there is no such agreement, the following provisions apply.

(3) The umpire shall attend the proceedings and be supplied with the same documents and other materials as are supplied to the other arbitrators.

(4) Decisions, orders and awards shall be made by the other arbitrators unless and until they cannot agree on a matter relating to the arbitration.

In that event they shall forthwith give notice in writing to the parties and the umpire, whereupon the umpire shall replace them as the tribunal with power to make decisions, orders and awards as if he were sole arbitrator.

(5) If the arbitrators cannot agree but fail to give notice of that fact, or if any of them fails to join in the giving of notice, any party to the arbitral proceedings may (upon notice to the other parties and to the tribunal) apply to the court which may order that the umpire shall replace the other arbitrators as the tribunal with power to make decisions, orders and awards as if he were sole arbitrator.

(6) The leave of the court is required for any appeal from a decision of the court under this section.

22.—(1) Where the parties agree that there shall be two or more arbitrators with no chairman or umpire, the parties are free to agree how the tribunal is to make decisions, orders and awards.

(2) If there is no such agreement, decisions, orders and awards shall be made by all or a majority of the arbitrators.

23.—(1) The parties are free to agree in what circumstances the authority of an arbitrator may be revoked.

(2) If or to the extent that there is no such agreement the following provisions apply.

(3) The authority of an arbitrator may not be revoked except—

    (a) by the parties acting jointly, or

    (b) by an arbitral or other institution or person vested by the parties with powers in that regard.

(4) Revocation of the authority of an arbitrator by the parties acting jointly must be agreed in writing unless the parties also agree (whether or not in writing) to terminate the arbitration agreement.

(5) Nothing in this section affects the power of the court—

    (a) to revoke an appointment under section 18 (powers exercisable in case of failure of appointment procedure), or

    (b) to remove an arbitrator on the grounds specified in section 24.

24.—(1) A party to arbitral proceedings may (upon notice to the other parties, to the arbitrator concerned and to any other arbitrator) apply to the court to remove an arbitrator on any of the following grounds—

    (a) that circumstances exist that give rise to justifiable doubts as to his impartiality;

    (b) that he does not possess the qualifications required by the arbitration agreement;

    (c) that he is physically or mentally incapable of conducting the proceedings or there are justifiable doubts as to his capacity to do so;

    (d) that he has refused or failed—

        (i) properly to conduct the proceedings, or

        (ii) to use all reasonable despatch in conducting the proceedings or making an award,

    and that substantial injustice has been or will be caused to the applicant.

(2) If there is an arbitral or other institution or person vested by the parties with power to remove an arbitrator, the court shall not exercise its power of removal unless satisfied that the applicant has first exhausted any available recourse to that institution or person.

(3) The arbitral tribunal may continue the arbitral proceedings and make an award while an application to the court under this section is pending.

(4) Where the court removes an arbitrator, it may make such order as it thinks fit with respect to his entitlement (if any) to fees or expenses, or the repayment of any fees or expenses already paid.

(5) The arbitrator concerned is entitled to appear and be heard by the court before it makes any order under this section.

(6) The leave of the court is required for any appeal from a decision of the court under this section.

Resignation of
arbitrator.

25.—(1) The parties are free to agree with an arbitrator as to the consequences of his resignation as regards—

(a) his entitlement (if any) to fees or expenses, and

(b) any liability thereby incurred by him.

(2) If or to the extent that there is no such agreement the following provisions apply.

(3) An arbitrator who resigns his appointment may (upon notice to the parties) apply to the court—

(a) to grant him relief from any liability thereby incurred by him, and

(b) to make such order as it thinks fit with respect to his entitlement (if any) to fees or expenses or the repayment of any fees or expenses already paid.

(4) If the court is satisfied that in all the circumstances it was reasonable for the arbitrator to resign, it may grant such relief as is mentioned in subsection (3)(a) on such terms as it thinks fit.

(5) The leave of the court is required for any appeal from a decision of the court under this section.

Death of
arbitrator or
person appointing
him.

26.—(1) The authority of an arbitrator is personal and ceases on his death.

(2) Unless otherwise agreed by the parties, the death of the person by whom an arbitrator was appointed does not revoke the arbitrator's authority.

Filling of vacancy,
&c.

27.—(1) Where an arbitrator ceases to hold office, the parties are free to agree—

(a) whether and if so how the vacancy is to be filled,

(b) whether and if so to what extent the previous proceedings should stand, and

(c) what effect (if any) his ceasing to hold office has on any appointment made by him (alone or jointly).

(2) If or to the extent that there is no such agreement, the following provisions apply.

(3) The provisions of sections 16 (procedure for appointment of arbitrators) and 18 (failure of appointment procedure) apply in relation to the filling of the vacancy as in relation to an original appointment.

(4) The tribunal (when reconstituted) shall determine whether and if so to what extent the previous proceedings should stand.

This does not affect any right of a party to challenge those proceedings on any ground which had arisen before the arbitrator ceased to hold office.

(5) His ceasing to hold office does not affect any appointment by him (alone or jointly) of another arbitrator, in particular any appointment of a chairman or umpire.

28.—(1) The parties are jointly and severally liable to pay to the arbitrators such reasonable fees and expenses (if any) as are appropriate in the circumstances.

Joint and several liability of parties to arbitrators for fees and expenses.

(2) Any party may apply to the court (upon notice to the other parties and to the arbitrators) which may order that the amount of the arbitrators' fees and expenses shall be considered and adjusted by such means and upon such terms as it may direct.

(3) If the application is made after any amount has been paid to the arbitrators by way of fees or expenses, the court may order the repayment of such amount (if any) as is shown to be excessive, but shall not do so unless it is shown that it is reasonable in the circumstances to order repayment.

(4) The above provisions have effect subject to any order of the court under section 24(4) or 25(3)(b) (order as to entitlement to fees or expenses in case of removal or resignation of arbitrator).

(5) Nothing in this section affects any liability of a party to any other party to pay all or any of the costs of the arbitration (see sections 59 to 65) or any contractual right of an arbitrator to payment of his fees and expenses.

(6) In this section references to arbitrators include an arbitrator who has ceased to act and an umpire who has not replaced the other arbitrators.

29.—(1) An arbitrator is not liable for anything done or omitted in the discharge or purported discharge of his functions as arbitrator unless the act or omission is shown to have been in bad faith.

Immunity of arbitrator.

(2) Subsection (1) applies to an employee or agent of an arbitrator as it applies to the arbitrator himself.

(3) This section does not affect any liability incurred by an arbitrator by reason of his resigning (but see section 25).

Jurisdiction of the arbitral tribunal

30.—(1) Unless otherwise agreed by the parties, the arbitral tribunal may rule on its own substantive jurisdiction, that is, as to—

Competence of tribunal to rule on its own jurisdiction.

(a) whether there is a valid arbitration agreement,

(b) whether the tribunal is properly constituted, and

(c) what matters have been submitted to arbitration in accordance with the arbitration agreement.

(2) Any such ruling may be challenged by any available arbitral process of appeal or review or in accordance with the provisions of this Part.

Objection to
substantive
jurisdiction of
tribunal.

31.—(1) An objection that the arbitral tribunal lacks substantive jurisdiction at the outset of the proceedings must be raised by a party not later than the time he takes the first step in the proceedings to contest the merits of any matter in relation to which he challenges the tribunal's jurisdiction.

A party is not precluded from raising such an objection by the fact that he has appointed or participated in the appointment of an arbitrator.

(2) Any objection during the course of the arbitral proceedings that the arbitral tribunal is exceeding its substantive jurisdiction must be made as soon as possible after the matter alleged to be beyond its jurisdiction is raised.

(3) The arbitral tribunal may admit an objection later than the time specified in subsection (1) or (2) if it considers the delay justified.

(4) Where an objection is duly taken to the tribunal's substantive jurisdiction and the tribunal has power to rule on its own jurisdiction, it may—

(a) rule on the matter in an award as to jurisdiction, or

(b) deal with the objection in its award on the merits.

If the parties agree which of these courses the tribunal should take, the tribunal shall proceed accordingly.

(5) The tribunal may in any case, and shall if the parties so agree, stay proceedings whilst an application is made to the court under section 32 (determination of preliminary point of jurisdiction).

Determination of
preliminary point
of jurisdiction.

32.—(1) The court may, on the application of a party to arbitral proceedings (upon notice to the other parties), determine any question as to the substantive jurisdiction of the tribunal.

A party may lose the right to object (see section 73).

(2) An application under this section shall not be considered unless—

(a) it is made with the agreement in writing of all the other parties to the proceedings, or

(b) it is made with the permission of the tribunal and the court is satisfied—

(i) that the determination of the question is likely to produce substantial savings in costs,

(ii) that the application was made without delay, and

(iii) that there is good reason why the matter should be decided by the court.

(3) An application under this section, unless made with the agreement of all the other parties to the proceedings, shall state the grounds on which it is said that the matter should be decided by the court.

(4) Unless otherwise agreed by the parties, the arbitral tribunal may continue the arbitral proceedings and make an award while an application to the court under this section is pending.

(5) Unless the court gives leave, no appeal lies from a decision of the court whether the conditions specified in subsection (2) are met.

(6) The decision of the court on the question of jurisdiction shall be treated as a judgment of the court for the purposes of an appeal.

But no appeal lies without the leave of the court which shall not be given unless the court considers that the question involves a point of law which is one of general importance or is one which for some other special reason should be considered by the Court of Appeal.

The arbitral proceedings

33.—(1) The tribunal shall—

General duty of the tribunal.

- (a) act fairly and impartially as between the parties, giving each party a reasonable opportunity of putting his case and dealing with that of his opponent, and

- (b) adopt procedures suitable to the circumstances of the particular case, avoiding unnecessary delay or expense, so as to provide a fair means for the resolution of the matters falling to be determined.

(2) The tribunal shall comply with that general duty in conducting the arbitral proceedings, in its decisions on matters of procedure and evidence and in the exercise of all other powers conferred on it.

34.—(1) It shall be for the tribunal to decide all procedural and evidential matters, subject to the right of the parties to agree any matter.

Procedural and evidential matters.

(2) Procedural and evidential matters include—

- (a) when and where any part of the proceedings is to be held;

- (b) the language or languages to be used in the proceedings and whether translations of any relevant documents are to be supplied;

- (c) whether any and if so what form of written statements of claim and defence are to be used, when these should be supplied and the extent to which such statements can be later amended;

- (d) whether any and if so which documents or classes of documents should be disclosed between and produced by the parties and at what stage;

- (e) whether any and if so what questions should be put to and answered by the respective parties and when and in what form this should be done;

- (f) whether to apply strict rules of evidence (or any other rules) as to the admissibility, relevance or weight of any material (oral, written or other) sought to be tendered on any matters of fact or opinion, and the time, manner and form in which such material should be exchanged and presented;

- (g) whether and to what extent the tribunal should itself take the initiative in ascertaining the facts and the law;

- (h) whether and to what extent there should be oral or written evidence or submissions.

(3) The tribunal may fix the time within which any directions given by it are to be complied with, and may if it thinks fit extend the time so fixed (whether or not it has expired).

Consolidation of proceedings and concurrent hearings.

35.—(1) The parties are free to agree—

(a) that the arbitral proceedings shall be consolidated with other arbitral proceedings, or

(b) that concurrent hearings shall be held,

on such terms as may be agreed.

(2) Unless the parties agree to confer such power on the tribunal, the tribunal has no power to order consolidation of proceedings or concurrent hearings.

Legal or other representation.

36. Unless otherwise agreed by the parties, a party to arbitral proceedings may be represented in the proceedings by a lawyer or other person chosen by him.

Power to appoint experts, legal advisers or assessors.

37.—(1) Unless otherwise agreed by the parties—

(a) the tribunal may—

(i) appoint experts or legal advisers to report to it and the parties, or

(ii) appoint assessors to assist it on technical matters,

and may allow any such expert, legal adviser or assessor to attend the proceedings; and

(b) the parties shall be given a reasonable opportunity to comment on any information, opinion or advice offered by any such person.

(2) The fees and expenses of an expert, legal adviser or assessor appointed by the tribunal for which the arbitrators are liable are expenses of the arbitrators for the purposes of this Part.

General powers exercisable by the tribunal.

38.—(1) The parties are free to agree on the powers exercisable by the arbitral tribunal for the purposes of and in relation to the proceedings.

(2) Unless otherwise agreed by the parties the tribunal has the following powers.

(3) The tribunal may order a claimant to provide security for the costs of the arbitration.

This power shall not be exercised on the ground that the claimant is—

(a) an individual ordinarily resident outside the United Kingdom, or

(b) a corporation or association incorporated or formed under the law of a country outside the United Kingdom, or whose central management and control is exercised outside the United Kingdom.

(4) The tribunal may give directions in relation to any property which is the subject of the proceedings or as to which any question arises in the proceedings, and which is owned by or is in the possession of a party to the proceedings—

(a) for the inspection, photographing, preservation, custody or detention of the property by the tribunal, an expert or a party, or

(b) ordering that samples be taken from, or any observation be made of or experiment conducted upon, the property.

(5) The tribunal may direct that a party or witness shall be examined on oath or affirmation, and may for that purpose administer any necessary oath or take any necessary affirmation.

(6) The tribunal may give directions to a party for the preservation for the purposes of the proceedings of any evidence in his custody or control.

39.—(1) The parties are free to agree that the tribunal shall have power to order on a provisional basis any relief which it would have power to grant in a final award.

Power to make provisional awards.

(2) This includes, for instance, making—

    (a) a provisional order for the payment of money or the disposition of property as between the parties, or

    (b) an order to make an interim payment on account of the costs of the arbitration.

(3) Any such order shall be subject to the tribunal's final adjudication; and the tribunal's final award, on the merits or as to costs, shall take account of any such order.

(4) Unless the parties agree to confer such power on the tribunal, the tribunal has no such power.

This does not affect its powers under section 47 (awards on different issues, &c.).

40.—(1) The parties shall do all things necessary for the proper and expeditious conduct of the arbitral proceedings.

General duty of parties.

(2) This includes—

    (a) complying without delay with any determination of the tribunal as to procedural or evidential matters, or with any order or directions of the tribunal, and

    (b) where appropriate, taking without delay any necessary steps to obtain a decision of the court on a preliminary question of jurisdiction or law (see sections 32 and 45).

41.—(1) The parties are free to agree on the powers of the tribunal in case of a party's failure to do something necessary for the proper and expeditious conduct of the arbitration.

Powers of tribunal in case of party's default.

(2) Unless otherwise agreed by the parties, the following provisions apply.

(3) If the tribunal is satisfied that there has been inordinate and inexcusable delay on the part of the claimant in pursuing his claim and that the delay—

    (a) gives rise, or is likely to give rise, to a substantial risk that it is not possible to have a fair resolution of the issues in that claim, or

    (b) has caused, or is likely to cause, serious prejudice to the respondent,

the tribunal may make an award dismissing the claim.

(4) If without showing sufficient cause a party—

(a) fails to attend or be represented at an oral hearing of which due notice was given, or

(b) where matters are to be dealt with in writing, fails after due notice to submit written evidence or make written submissions,

the tribunal may continue the proceedings in the absence of that party or, as the case may be, without any written evidence or submissions on his behalf, and may make an award on the basis of the evidence before it.

(5) If without showing sufficient cause a party fails to comply with any order or directions of the tribunal, the tribunal may make a peremptory order to the same effect, prescribing such time for compliance with it as the tribunal considers appropriate.

(6) If a claimant fails to comply with a peremptory order of the tribunal to provide security for costs, the tribunal may make an award dismissing his claim.

(7) If a party fails to comply with any other kind of peremptory order, then, without prejudice to section 42 (enforcement by court of tribunal's peremptory orders), the tribunal may do any of the following—

(a) direct that the party in default shall not be entitled to rely upon any allegation or material which was the subject matter of the order;

(b) draw such adverse inferences from the act of non-compliance as the circumstances justify;

(c) proceed to an award on the basis of such materials as have been properly provided to it;

(d) make such order as it thinks fit as to the payment of costs of the arbitration incurred in consequence of the non-compliance.

Powers of court in relation to arbitral proceedings

Enforcement of peremptory orders of tribunal.

42.—(1) Unless otherwise agreed by the parties, the court may make an order requiring a party to comply with a peremptory order made by the tribunal.

(2) An application for an order under this section may be made—

(a) by the tribunal (upon notice to the parties),

(b) by a party to the arbitral proceedings with the permission of the tribunal (and upon notice to the other parties), or

(c) where the parties have agreed that the powers of the court under this section shall be available.

(3) The court shall not act unless it is satisfied that the applicant has exhausted any available arbitral process in respect of failure to comply with the tribunal's order.

(4) No order shall be made under this section unless the court is satisfied that the person to whom the tribunal's order was directed has failed to comply with it within the time prescribed in the order or, if no time was prescribed, within a reasonable time.

(5) The leave of the court is required for any appeal from a decision of the court under this section.

43.—(1) A party to arbitral proceedings may use the same court procedures as are available in relation to legal proceedings to secure the attendance before the tribunal of a witness in order to give oral testimony or to produce documents or other material evidence.

(2) This may only be done with the permission of the tribunal or the agreement of the other parties.

(3) The court procedures may only be used if—

    (a) the witness is in the United Kingdom, and

    (b) the arbitral proceedings are being conducted in England and Wales or, as the case may be, Northern Ireland.

(4) A person shall not be compelled by virtue of this section to produce any document or other material evidence which he could not be compelled to produce in legal proceedings.

44.—(1) Unless otherwise agreed by the parties, the court has for the purposes of and in relation to arbitral proceedings the same power of making orders about the matters listed below as it has for the purposes of and in relation to legal proceedings.

(2) Those matters are—

    (a) the taking of the evidence of witnesses;

    (b) the preservation of evidence;

    (c) making orders relating to property which is the subject of the proceedings or as to which any question arises in the proceedings—

        (i) for the inspection, photographing, preservation, custody or detention of the property, or

        (ii) ordering that samples be taken from, or any observation be made of or experiment conducted upon, the property;

    and for that purpose authorising any person to enter any premises in the possession or control of a party to the arbitration;

    (d) the sale of any goods the subject of the proceedings;

    (e) the granting of an interim injunction or the appointment of a receiver.

(3) If the case is one of urgency, the court may, on the application of a party or proposed party to the arbitral proceedings, make such orders as it thinks necessary for the purpose of preserving evidence or assets.

(4) If the case is not one of urgency, the court shall act only on the application of a party to the arbitral proceedings (upon notice to the other parties and to the tribunal) made with the permission of the tribunal or the agreement in writing of the other parties.

(5) In any case the court shall act only if or to the extent that the arbitral tribunal, and any arbitral or other institution or person vested by the parties with power in that regard, has no power or is unable for the time being to act effectively.

PART I

(6) If the court so orders, an order made by it under this section shall cease to have effect in whole or in part on the order of the tribunal or of any such arbitral or other institution or person having power to act in relation to the subject-matter of the order.

(7) The leave of the court is required for any appeal from a decision of the court under this section.

Determination of preliminary point of law.

45.—(1) Unless otherwise agreed by the parties, the court may on the application of a party to arbitral proceedings (upon notice to the other parties) determine any question of law arising in the course of the proceedings which the court is satisfied substantially affects the rights of one or more of the parties.

An agreement to dispense with reasons for the tribunal's award shall be considered an agreement to exclude the court's jurisdiction under this section.

(2) An application under this section shall not be considered unless—

    (a) it is made with the agreement of all the other parties to the proceedings, or

    (b) it is made with the permission of the tribunal and the court is satisfied—

        (i) that the determination of the question is likely to produce substantial savings in costs, and

        (ii) that the application was made without delay.

(3) The application shall identify the question of law to be determined and, unless made with the agreement of all the other parties to the proceedings, shall state the grounds on which it is said that the question should be decided by the court.

(4) Unless otherwise agreed by the parties, the arbitral tribunal may continue the arbitral proceedings and make an award while an application to the court under this section is pending.

(5) Unless the court gives leave, no appeal lies from a decision of the court whether the conditions specified in subsection (2) are met.

(6) The decision of the court on the question of law shall be treated as a judgment of the court for the purposes of an appeal.

But no appeal lies without the leave of the court which shall not be given unless the court considers that the question is one of general importance, or is one which for some other special reason should be considered by the Court of Appeal.

The award

Rules applicable to substance of dispute.

46.—(1) The arbitral tribunal shall decide the dispute—

    (a) in accordance with the law chosen by the parties as applicable to the substance of the dispute, or

    (b) if the parties so agree, in accordance with such other considerations as are agreed by them or determined by the tribunal.

(2) For this purpose the choice of the laws of a country shall be understood to refer to the substantive laws of that country and not its conflict of laws rules.

(3) If or to the extent that there is no such choice or agreement, the tribunal shall apply the law determined by the conflict of laws rules which it considers applicable.

47.—(1) Unless otherwise agreed by the parties, the tribunal may make more than one award at different times on different aspects of the matters to be determined.

(2) The tribunal may, in particular, make an award relating—

(a) to an issue affecting the whole claim, or

(b) to a part only of the claims or cross-claims submitted to it for decision.

(3) If the tribunal does so, it shall specify in its award the issue, or the claim or part of a claim, which is the subject matter of the award.

48.—(1) The parties are free to agree on the powers exercisable by the arbitral tribunal as regards remedies.

(2) Unless otherwise agreed by the parties, the tribunal has the following powers.

(3) The tribunal may make a declaration as to any matter to be determined in the proceedings.

(4) The tribunal may order the payment of a sum of money, in any currency.

(5) The tribunal has the same powers as the court—

(a) to order a party to do or refrain from doing anything;

(b) to order specific performance of a contract (other than a contract relating to land);

(c) to order the rectification, setting aside or cancellation of a deed or other document.

49.—(1) The parties are free to agree on the powers of the tribunal as regards the award of interest.

(2) Unless otherwise agreed by the parties the following provisions apply.

(3) The tribunal may award simple or compound interest from such dates, at such rates and with such rests as it considers meets the justice of the case—

(a) on the whole or part of any amount awarded by the tribunal, in respect of any period up to the date of the award;

(b) on the whole or part of any amount claimed in the arbitration and outstanding at the commencement of the arbitral proceedings but paid before the award was made, in respect of any period up to the date of payment.

(4) The tribunal may award simple or compound interest from the date of the award (or any later date) until payment, at such rates and with such rests as it considers meets the justice of the case, on the outstanding amount of any award (including any award of interest under subsection (3) and any award as to costs).

(5) References in this section to an amount awarded by the tribunal include an amount payable in consequence of a declaratory award by the tribunal.

(6) The above provisions do not affect any other power of the tribunal to award interest.

Extension of time for making award.

50.—(1) Where the time for making an award is limited by or in pursuance of the arbitration agreement, then, unless otherwise agreed by the parties, the court may in accordance with the following provisions by order extend that time.

(2) An application for an order under this section may be made—

(a) by the tribunal (upon notice to the parties), or

(b) by any party to the proceedings (upon notice to the tribunal and the other parties),

but only after exhausting any available arbitral process for obtaining an extension of time.

(3) The court shall only make an order if satisfied that a substantial injustice would otherwise be done.

(4) The court may extend the time for such period and on such terms as it thinks fit, and may do so whether or not the time previously fixed (by or under the agreement or by a previous order) has expired.

(5) The leave of the court is required for any appeal from a decision of the court under this section.

Settlement.

51.—(1) If during arbitral proceedings the parties settle the dispute, the following provisions apply unless otherwise agreed by the parties.

(2) The tribunal shall terminate the substantive proceedings and, if so requested by the parties and not objected to by the tribunal, shall record the settlement in the form of an agreed award.

(3) An agreed award shall state that it is an award of the tribunal and shall have the same status and effect as any other award on the merits of the case.

(4) The following provisions of this Part relating to awards (sections 52 to 58) apply to an agreed award.

(5) Unless the parties have also settled the matter of the payment of the costs of the arbitration, the provisions of this Part relating to costs (sections 59 to 65) continue to apply.

Form of award.

52.—(1) The parties are free to agree on the form of an award.

(2) If or to the extent that there is no such agreement, the following provisions apply.

(3) The award shall be in writing signed by all the arbitrators or all those assenting to the award.

(4) The award shall contain the reasons for the award unless it is an agreed award or the parties have agreed to dispense with reasons.

(5) The award shall state the seat of the arbitration and the date when the award is made.

53. Unless otherwise agreed by the parties, where the seat of the arbitration is in England and Wales or Northern Ireland, any award in the proceedings shall be treated as made there, regardless of where it was signed, despatched or delivered to any of the parties.

54.—(1) Unless otherwise agreed by the parties, the tribunal may decide what is to be taken to be the date on which the award was made.

(2) In the absence of any such decision, the date of the award shall be taken to be the date on which it is signed by the arbitrator or, where more than one arbitrator signs the award, by the last of them.

55.—(1) The parties are free to agree on the requirements as to notification of the award to the parties.

(2) If there is no such agreement, the award shall be notified to the parties by service on them of copies of the award, which shall be done without delay after the award is made.

(3) Nothing in this section affects section 56 (power to withhold award in case of non-payment).

56.—(1) The tribunal may refuse to deliver an award to the parties except upon full payment of the fees and expenses of the arbitrators.

(2) If the tribunal refuses on that ground to deliver an award, a party to the arbitral proceedings may (upon notice to the other parties and the tribunal) apply to the court, which may order that—

    (a) the tribunal shall deliver the award on the payment into court by the applicant of the fees and expenses demanded, or such lesser amount as the court may specify,

    (b) the amount of the fees and expenses properly payable shall be determined by such means and upon such terms as the court may direct, and

    (c) out of the money paid into court there shall be paid out such fees and expenses as may be found to be properly payable and the balance of the money (if any) shall be paid out to the applicant.

(3) For this purpose the amount of fees and expenses properly payable is the amount the applicant is liable to pay under section 28 or any agreement relating to the payment of the arbitrators.

(4) No application to the court may be made where there is any available arbitral process for appeal or review of the amount of the fees or expenses demanded.

(5) References in this section to arbitrators include an arbitrator who has ceased to act and an umpire who has not replaced the other arbitrators.

(6) The above provisions of this section also apply in relation to any arbitral or other institution or person vested by the parties with powers in relation to the delivery of the tribunal's award.

As they so apply, the references to the fees and expenses of the arbitrators shall be construed as including the fees and expenses of that institution or person.

(7) The leave of the court is required for any appeal from a decision of the court under this section.

(8) Nothing in this section shall be construed as excluding an application under section 28 where payment has been made to the arbitrators in order to obtain the award.

Correction of award or additional award.

57.—(1) The parties are free to agree on the powers of the tribunal to correct an award or make an additional award.

(2) If or to the extent there is no such agreement, the following provisions apply.

(3) The tribunal may on its own initiative or on the application of a party—

(a) correct an award so as to remove any clerical mistake or error arising from an accidental slip or omission or clarify or remove any ambiguity in the award, or

(b) make an additional award in respect of any claim (including a claim for interest or costs) which was presented to the tribunal but was not dealt with in the award.

These powers shall not be exercised without first affording the other parties a reasonable opportunity to make representations to the tribunal.

(4) Any application for the exercise of those powers must be made within 28 days of the date of the award or such longer period as the parties may agree.

(5) Any correction of an award shall be made within 28 days of the date the application was received by the tribunal or, where the correction is made by the tribunal on its own initiative, within 28 days of the date of the award or, in either case, such longer period as the parties may agree.

(6) Any additional award shall be made within 56 days of the date of the original award or such longer period as the parties may agree.

(7) Any correction of an award shall form part of the award.

Effect of award.

58.—(1) Unless otherwise agreed by the parties, an award made by the tribunal pursuant to an arbitration agreement is final and binding both on the parties and on any persons claiming through or under them.

(2) This does not affect the right of a person to challenge the award by any available arbitral process of appeal or review or in accordance with the provisions of this Part.

Costs of the arbitration

Costs of the arbitration.

59.—(1) References in this Part to the costs of the arbitration are to—

(a) the arbitrators' fees and expenses,

(b) the fees and expenses of any arbitral institution concerned, and

(c) the legal or other costs of the parties.

(2) Any such reference includes the costs of or incidental to any proceedings to determine the amount of the recoverable costs of the arbitration (see section 63).

60. An agreement which has the effect that a party is to pay the whole or part of the costs of the arbitration in any event is only valid if made after the dispute in question has arisen.

Agreement to pay costs in any event.

61.—(1) The tribunal may make an award allocating the costs of the arbitration as between the parties, subject to any agreement of the parties.

Award of costs.

(2) Unless the parties otherwise agree, the tribunal shall award costs on the general principle that costs should follow the event except where it appears to the tribunal that in the circumstances this is not appropriate in relation to the whole or part of the costs.

62. Unless the parties otherwise agree, any obligation under an agreement between them as to how the costs of the arbitration are to be borne, or under an award allocating the costs of the arbitration, extends only to such costs as are recoverable.

Effect of agreement or award about costs.

63.—(1) The parties are free to agree what costs of the arbitration are recoverable.

The recoverable costs of the arbitration.

(2) If or to the extent there is no such agreement, the following provisions apply.

(3) The tribunal may determine by award the recoverable costs of the arbitration on such basis as it thinks fit.

If it does so, it shall specify—

(a) the basis on which it has acted, and

(b) the items of recoverable costs and the amount referable to each.

(4) If the tribunal does not determine the recoverable costs of the arbitration, any party to the arbitral proceedings may apply to the court (upon notice to the other parties) which may—

(a) determine the recoverable costs of the arbitration on such basis as it thinks fit, or

(b) order that they shall be determined by such means and upon such terms as it may specify.

(5) Unless the tribunal or the court determines otherwise—

(a) the recoverable costs of the arbitration shall be determined on the basis that there shall be allowed a reasonable amount in respect of all costs reasonably incurred, and

(b) any doubt as to whether costs were reasonably incurred or were reasonable in amount shall be resolved in favour of the paying party.

(6) The above provisions have effect subject to section 64 (recoverable fees and expenses of arbitrators).

(7) Nothing in this section affects any right of the arbitrators, any expert, legal adviser or assessor appointed by the tribunal, or any arbitral institution, to payment of their fees and expenses.

64.—(1) Unless otherwise agreed by the parties, the recoverable costs of the arbitration shall include in respect of the fees and expenses of the arbitrators only such reasonable fees and expenses as are appropriate in the circumstances.

Recoverable fees and expenses of arbitrators.

(2) If there is any question as to what reasonable fees and expenses are appropriate in the circumstances, and the matter is not already before the court on an application under section 63(4), the court may on the application of any party (upon notice to the other parties)—

(a) determine the matter, or

(b) order that it be determined by such means and upon such terms as the court may specify.

(3) Subsection (1) has effect subject to any order of the court under section 24(4) or 25(3)(b) (order as to entitlement to fees or expenses in case of removal or resignation of arbitrator).

(4) Nothing in this section affects any right of the arbitrator to payment of his fees and expenses.

Power to limit recoverable costs.

65.—(1) Unless otherwise agreed by the parties, the tribunal may direct that the recoverable costs of the arbitration, or of any part of the arbitral proceedings, shall be limited to a specified amount.

(2) Any direction may be made or varied at any stage, but this must be done sufficiently in advance of the incurring of costs to which it relates, or the taking of any steps in the proceedings which may be affected by it, for the limit to be taken into account.

Powers of the court in relation to award

Enforcement of the award.

66.—(1) An award made by the tribunal pursuant to an arbitration agreement may, by leave of the court, be enforced in the same manner as a judgment or order of the court to the same effect.

(2) Where leave is so given, judgment may be entered in terms of the award.

(3) Leave to enforce an award shall not be given where, or to the extent that, the person against whom it is sought to be enforced shows that the tribunal lacked substantive jurisdiction to make the award.

The right to raise such an objection may have been lost (see section 73).

1950 c. 27.

(4) Nothing in this section affects the recognition or enforcement of an award under any other enactment or rule of law, in particular under Part II of the Arbitration Act 1950 (enforcement of awards under Geneva Convention) or the provisions of Part III of this Act relating to the recognition and enforcement of awards under the New York Convention or by an action on the award.

Challenging the award: substantive jurisdiction.

67.—(1) A party to arbitral proceedings may (upon notice to the other parties and to the tribunal) apply to the court—

(a) challenging any award of the arbitral tribunal as to its substantive jurisdiction; or

(b) for an order declaring an award made by the tribunal on the merits to be of no effect, in whole or in part, because the tribunal did not have substantive jurisdiction.

A party may lose the right to object (see section 73) and the right to apply is subject to the restrictions in section 70(2) and (3).

(2) The arbitral tribunal may continue the arbitral proceedings and make a further award while an application to the court under this section is pending in relation to an award as to jurisdiction.

(3) On an application under this section challenging an award of the arbitral tribunal as to its substantive jurisdiction, the court may by order—

    (a) confirm the award,

    (b) vary the award, or

    (c) set aside the award in whole or in part.

(4) The leave of the court is required for any appeal from a decision of the court under this section.

68.—(1) A party to arbitral proceedings may (upon notice to the other parties and to the tribunal) apply to the court challenging an award in the proceedings on the ground of serious irregularity affecting the tribunal, the proceedings or the award.

Challenging the
award: serious
irregularity.

A party may lose the right to object (see section 73) and the right to apply is subject to the restrictions in section 70(2) and (3).

(2) Serious irregularity means an irregularity of one or more of the following kinds which the court considers has caused or will cause substantial injustice to the applicant—

    (a) failure by the tribunal to comply with section 33 (general duty of tribunal);

    (b) the tribunal exceeding its powers (otherwise than by exceeding its substantive jurisdiction: see section 67);

    (c) failure by the tribunal to conduct the proceedings in accordance with the procedure agreed by the parties;

    (d) failure by the tribunal to deal with all the issues that were put to it;

    (e) any arbitral or other institution or person vested by the parties with powers in relation to the proceedings or the award exceeding its powers;

    (f) uncertainty or ambiguity as to the effect of the award;

    (g) the award being obtained by fraud or the award or the way in which it was procured being contrary to public policy;

    (h) failure to comply with the requirements as to the form of the award; or

    (i) any irregularity in the conduct of the proceedings or in the award which is admitted by the tribunal or by any arbitral or other institution or person vested by the parties with powers in relation to the proceedings or the award.

(3) If there is shown to be serious irregularity affecting the tribunal, the proceedings or the award, the court may—

    (a) remit the award to the tribunal, in whole or in part, for reconsideration,

    (b) set the award aside in whole or in part, or

    (c) declare the award to be of no effect, in whole or in part.

The court shall not exercise its power to set aside or to declare an award to be of no effect, in whole or in part, unless it is satisfied that it would be inappropriate to remit the matters in question to the tribunal for reconsideration.

(4) The leave of the court is required for any appeal from a decision of the court under this section.

Appeal on point of law.

69.—(1) Unless otherwise agreed by the parties, a party to arbitral proceedings may (upon notice to the other parties and to the tribunal) appeal to the court on a question of law arising out of an award made in the proceedings.

An agreement to dispense with reasons for the tribunal's award shall be considered an agreement to exclude the court's jurisdiction under this section.

(2) An appeal shall not be brought under this section except—

(a) with the agreement of all the other parties to the proceedings, or

(b) with the leave of the court.

The right to appeal is also subject to the restrictions in section 70(2) and (3).

(3) Leave to appeal shall be given only if the court is satisfied—

(a) that the determination of the question will substantially affect the rights of one or more of the parties,

(b) that the question is one which the tribunal was asked to determine,

(c) that, on the basis of the findings of fact in the award—

(i) the decision of the tribunal on the question is obviously wrong, or

(ii) the question is one of general public importance and the decision of the tribunal is at least open to serious doubt, and

(d) that, despite the agreement of the parties to resolve the matter by arbitration, it is just and proper in all the circumstances for the court to determine the question.

(4) An application for leave to appeal under this section shall identify the question of law to be determined and state the grounds on which it is alleged that leave to appeal should be granted.

(5) The court shall determine an application for leave to appeal under this section without a hearing unless it appears to the court that a hearing is required.

(6) The leave of the court is required for any appeal from a decision of the court under this section to grant or refuse leave to appeal.

(7) On an appeal under this section the court may by order—

(a) confirm the award,

(b) vary the award,

(c) remit the award to the tribunal, in whole or in part, for reconsideration in the light of the court's determination, or

(d) set aside the award in whole or in part.

The court shall not exercise its power to set aside an award, in whole or in part, unless it is satisfied that it would be inappropriate to remit the matters in question to the tribunal for reconsideration.

(8) The decision of the court on an appeal under this section shall be treated as a judgment of the court for the purposes of a further appeal.

But no such appeal lies without the leave of the court which shall not be given unless the court considers that the question is one of general importance or is one which for some other special reason should be considered by the Court of Appeal.

70.—(1) The following provisions apply to an application or appeal under section 67, 68 or 69.

(2) An application or appeal may not be brought if the applicant or appellant has not first exhausted—

Challenge or appeal: supplementary provisions.

(a) any available arbitral process of appeal or review, and

(b) any available recourse under section 57 (correction of award or additional award).

(3) Any application or appeal must be brought within 28 days of the date of the award or, if there has been any arbitral process of appeal or review, of the date when the applicant or appellant was notified of the result of that process.

(4) If on an application or appeal it appears to the court that the award—

(a) does not contain the tribunal's reasons, or

(b) does not set out the tribunal's reasons in sufficient detail to enable the court properly to consider the application or appeal,

the court may order the tribunal to state the reasons for its award in sufficient detail for that purpose.

(5) Where the court makes an order under subsection (4), it may make such further order as it thinks fit with respect to any additional costs of the arbitration resulting from its order.

(6) The court may order the applicant or appellant to provide security for the costs of the application or appeal, and may direct that the application or appeal be dismissed if the order is not complied with.

The power to order security for costs shall not be exercised on the ground that the applicant or appellant is—

(a) an individual ordinarily resident outside the United Kingdom, or

(b) a corporation or association incorporated or formed under the law of a country outside the United Kingdom, or whose central management and control is exercised outside the United Kingdom.

(7) The court may order that any money payable under the award shall be brought into court or otherwise secured pending the determination of the application or appeal, and may direct that the application or appeal be dismissed if the order is not complied with.

(8) The court may grant leave to appeal subject to conditions to the same or similar effect as an order under subsection (6) or (7).

This does not affect the general discretion of the court to grant leave subject to conditions.

Challenge or
appeal: effect of
order of court.

71.—(1) The following provisions have effect where the court makes an order under section 67, 68 or 69 with respect to an award.

(2) Where the award is varied, the variation has effect as part of the tribunal's award.

(3) Where the award is remitted to the tribunal, in whole or in part, for reconsideration, the tribunal shall make a fresh award in respect of the matters remitted within three months of the date of the order for remission or such longer or shorter period as the court may direct.

(4) Where the award is set aside or declared to be of no effect, in whole or in part, the court may also order that any provision that an award is a condition precedent to the bringing of legal proceedings in respect of a matter to which the arbitration agreement applies, is of no effect as regards the subject matter of the award or, as the case may be, the relevant part of the award.

Miscellaneous

Saving for rights
of person who
takes no part in
proceedings.

72.—(1) A person alleged to be a party to arbitral proceedings but who takes no part in the proceedings may question—

(a) whether there is a valid arbitration agreement,

(b) whether the tribunal is properly constituted, or

(c) what matters have been submitted to arbitration in accordance with the arbitration agreement,

by proceedings in the court for a declaration or injunction or other appropriate relief.

(2) He also has the same right as a party to the arbitral proceedings to challenge an award—

(a) by an application under section 67 on the ground of lack of substantive jurisdiction in relation to him, or

(b) by an application under section 68 on the ground of serious irregularity (within the meaning of that section) affecting him;

and section 70(2) (duty to exhaust arbitral procedures) does not apply in his case.

Loss of right to
object.

73.—(1) If a party to arbitral proceedings takes part, or continues to take part, in the proceedings without making, either forthwith or within such time as is allowed by the arbitration agreement or the tribunal or by any provision of this Part, any objection—

(a) that the tribunal lacks substantive jurisdiction,

(b) that the proceedings have been improperly conducted,

(c) that there has been a failure to comply with the arbitration agreement or with any provision of this Part, or

    (d) that there has been any other irregularity affecting the tribunal or the proceedings,

he may not raise that objection later, before the tribunal or the court, unless he shows that, at the time he took part or continued to take part in the proceedings, he did not know and could not with reasonable diligence have discovered the grounds for the objection.

(2) Where the arbitral tribunal rules that it has substantive jurisdiction and a party to arbitral proceedings who could have questioned that ruling—

    (a) by any available arbitral process of appeal or review, or

    (b) by challenging the award,

does not do so, or does not do so within the time allowed by the arbitration agreement or any provision of this Part, he may not object later to the tribunal's substantive jurisdiction on any ground which was the subject of that ruling.

74.—(1) An arbitral or other institution or person designated or requested by the parties to appoint or nominate an arbitrator is not liable for anything done or omitted in the discharge or purported discharge of that function unless the act or omission is shown to have been in bad faith.

Immunity of arbitral institutions, &c.

(2) An arbitral or other institution or person by whom an arbitrator is appointed or nominated is not liable, by reason of having appointed or nominated him, for anything done or omitted by the arbitrator (or his employees or agents) in the discharge or purported discharge of his functions as arbitrator.

(3) The above provisions apply to an employee or agent of an arbitral or other institution or person as they apply to the institution or person himself.

75. The powers of the court to make declarations and orders under section 73 of the Solicitors Act 1974 or Article 71H of the Solicitors (Northern Ireland) Order 1976 (power to charge property recovered in the proceedings with the payment of solicitors' costs) may be exercised in relation to arbitral proceedings as if those proceedings were proceedings in the court.

Charge to secure payment of solicitors' costs.
1974 c. 47.
S.I. 1976/582 (N.I. 12).

Supplementary

76.—(1) The parties are free to agree on the manner of service of any notice or other document required or authorised to be given or served in pursuance of the arbitration agreement or for the purposes of the arbitral proceedings.

Service of notices, &c.

(2) If or to the extent that there is no such agreement the following provisions apply.

(3) A notice or other document may be served on a person by any effective means.

(4) If a notice or other document is addressed, pre-paid and delivered by post—

    (a) to the addressee's last known principal residence or, if he is or has been carrying on a trade, profession or business, his last known principal business address, or

(b) where the addressee is a body corporate, to the body's registered or principal office,

it shall be treated as effectively served.

(5) This section does not apply to the service of documents for the purposes of legal proceedings, for which provision is made by rules of court.

(6) References in this Part to a notice or other document include any form of communication in writing and references to giving or serving a notice or other document shall be construed accordingly.

Powers of court in relation to service of documents.

77.—(1) This section applies where service of a document on a person in the manner agreed by the parties, or in accordance with provisions of section 76 having effect in default of agreement, is not reasonably practicable.

(2) Unless otherwise agreed by the parties, the court may make such order as it thinks fit—

(a) for service in such manner as the court may direct, or

(b) dispensing with service of the document.

(3) Any party to the arbitration agreement may apply for an order, but only after exhausting any available arbitral process for resolving the matter.

(4) The leave of the court is required for any appeal from a decision of the court under this section.

Reckoning periods of time.

78.—(1) The parties are free to agree on the method of reckoning periods of time for the purposes of any provision agreed by them or any provision of this Part having effect in default of such agreement.

(2) If or to the extent there is no such agreement, periods of time shall be reckoned in accordance with the following provisions.

(3) Where the act is required to be done within a specified period after or from a specified date, the period begins immediately after that date.

(4) Where the act is required to be done a specified number of clear days after a specified date, at least that number of days must intervene between the day on which the act is done and that date.

(5) Where the period is a period of seven days or less which would include a Saturday, Sunday or a public holiday in the place where anything which has to be done within the period falls to be done, that day shall be excluded.

In relation to England and Wales or Northern Ireland, a "public holiday" means Christmas Day, Good Friday or a day which under the Banking and Financial Dealings Act 1971 is a bank holiday.

1971 c. 80.

Power of court to extend time limits relating to arbitral proceedings.

79.—(1) Unless the parties otherwise agree, the court may by order extend any time limit agreed by them in relation to any matter relating to the arbitral proceedings or specified in any provision of this Part having effect in default of such agreement.

This section does not apply to a time limit to which section 12 applies (power of court to extend time for beginning arbitral proceedings, &c.).

(2) An application for an order may be made—

    (a) by any party to the arbitral proceedings (upon notice to the other parties and to the tribunal), or

    (b) by the arbitral tribunal (upon notice to the parties).

(3) The court shall not exercise its power to extend a time limit unless it is satisfied—

    (a) that any available recourse to the tribunal, or to any arbitral or other institution or person vested by the parties with power in that regard, has first been exhausted, and

    (b) that a substantial injustice would otherwise be done.

(4) The court's power under this section may be exercised whether or not the time has already expired.

(5) An order under this section may be made on such terms as the court thinks fit.

(6) The leave of the court is required for any appeal from a decision of the court under this section.

80.—(1) References in this Part to an application, appeal or other step in relation to legal proceedings being taken "upon notice" to the other parties to the arbitral proceedings, or to the tribunal, are to such notice of the originating process as is required by rules of court and do not impose any separate requirement.

Notice and other requirements in connection with legal proceedings.

(2) Rules of court shall be made—

    (a) requiring such notice to be given as indicated by any provision of this Part, and

    (b) as to the manner, form and content of any such notice.

(3) Subject to any provision made by rules of court, a requirement to give notice to the tribunal of legal proceedings shall be construed—

    (a) if there is more than one arbitrator, as a requirement to give notice to each of them; and

    (b) if the tribunal is not fully constituted, as a requirement to give notice to any arbitrator who has been appointed.

(4) References in this Part to making an application or appeal to the court within a specified period are to the issue within that period of the appropriate originating process in accordance with rules of court.

(5) Where any provision of this Part requires an application or appeal to be made to the court within a specified time, the rules of court relating to the reckoning of periods, the extending or abridging of periods, and the consequences of not taking a step within the period prescribed by the rules, apply in relation to that requirement.

(6) Provision may be made by rules of court amending the provisions of this Part—

    (a) with respect to the time within which any application or appeal to the court must be made,

    (b) so as to keep any provision made by this Part in relation to arbitral proceedings in step with the corresponding provision of rules of court applying in relation to proceedings in the court, or

PART I

(c) so as to keep any provision made by this Part in relation to legal proceedings in step with the corresponding provision of rules of court applying generally in relation to proceedings in the court.

(7) Nothing in this section affects the generality of the power to make rules of court.

Saving for certain matters governed by common law.

81.—(1) Nothing in this Part shall be construed as excluding the operation of any rule of law consistent with the provisions of this Part, in particular, any rule of law as to—

(a) matters which are not capable of settlement by arbitration;

(b) the effect of an oral arbitration agreement; or

(c) the refusal of recognition or enforcement of an arbitral award on grounds of public policy.

(2) Nothing in this Act shall be construed as reviving any jurisdiction of the court to set aside or remit an award on the ground of errors of fact or law on the face of the award.

Minor definitions.

82.—(1) In this Part—

"arbitrator", unless the context otherwise requires, includes an umpire;

"available arbitral process", in relation to any matter, includes any process of appeal to or review by an arbitral or other institution or person vested by the parties with powers in relation to that matter;

"claimant", unless the context otherwise requires, includes a counterclaimant, and related expressions shall be construed accordingly;

"dispute" includes any difference;

"enactment" includes an enactment contained in Northern Ireland legislation;

"legal proceedings" means civil proceedings in the High Court or a county court;

"peremptory order" means an order made under section 41(5) or made in exercise of any corresponding power conferred by the parties;

"premises" includes land, buildings, moveable structures, vehicles, vessels, aircraft and hovercraft;

"question of law" means—

(a) for a court in England and Wales, a question of the law of England and Wales, and

(b) for a court in Northern Ireland, a question of the law of Northern Ireland;

"substantive jurisdiction", in relation to an arbitral tribunal, refers to the matters specified in section 30(1)(a) to (c), and references to the tribunal exceeding its substantive jurisdiction shall be construed accordingly.

(2) References in this Part to a party to an arbitration agreement include any person claiming under or through a party to the agreement.

83. In this Part the expressions listed below are defined or otherwise explained by the provisions indicated—

agreement, agree and agreed	section 5(1)
agreement in writing	section 5(2) to (5)
arbitration agreement	sections 6 and 5(1)
arbitrator	section 82(1)
available arbitral process	section 82(1)
claimant	section 82(1)
commencement (in relation to arbitral proceedings)	section 14
costs of the arbitration	section 59
the court	section 105
dispute	section 82(1)
enactment	section 82(1)
legal proceedings	section 82(1)
Limitation Acts	section 13(4)
notice (or other document)	section 76(6)
party—	
—in relation to an arbitration agreement	section 82(2)
—where section 106(2) or (3) applies	section 106(4)
peremptory order	section 82(1) (and see section 41(5))
premises	section 82(1)
question of law	section 82(1)
recoverable costs	sections 63 and 64
seat of the arbitration	section 3
serve and service (of notice or other document)	section 76(6)
substantive jurisdiction (in relation to an arbitral tribunal)	section 82(1) (and see section 30(1)(a) to (c))
upon notice (to the parties or the tribunal)	section 80
written and in writing	section 5(6)

84.—(1) The provisions of this Part do not apply to arbitral proceedings commenced before the date on which this Part comes into force.

(2) They apply to arbitral proceedings commenced on or after that date under an arbitration agreement whenever made.

(3) The above provisions have effect subject to any transitional provision made by an order under section 109(2) (power to include transitional provisions in commencement order).

Part II

Other provisions relating to arbitration

Domestic arbitration agreements

85.—(1) In the case of a domestic arbitration agreement the provisions of Part I are modified in accordance with the following sections.

(2) For this purpose a "domestic arbitration agreement" means an arbitration agreement to which none of the parties is—

(a) an individual who is a national of, or habitually resident in, a state other than the United Kingdom, or

(b) a body corporate which is incorporated in, or whose central control and management is exercised in, a state other than the United Kingdom,

and under which the seat of the arbitration (if the seat has been designated or determined) is in the United Kingdom.

(3) In subsection (2) "arbitration agreement" and "seat of the arbitration" have the same meaning as in Part I (see sections 3, 5(1) and 6).

Staying of legal proceedings.

86.—(1) In section 9 (stay of legal proceedings), subsection (4) (stay unless the arbitration agreement is null and void, inoperative, or incapable of being performed) does not apply to a domestic arbitration agreement.

(2) On an application under that section in relation to a domestic arbitration agreement the court shall grant a stay unless satisfied—

(a) that the arbitration agreement is null and void, inoperative, or incapable of being performed, or

(b) that there are other sufficient grounds for not requiring the parties to abide by the arbitration agreement.

(3) The court may treat as a sufficient ground under subsection (2)(b) the fact that the applicant is or was at any material time not ready and willing to do all things necessary for the proper conduct of the arbitration or of any other dispute resolution procedures required to be exhausted before resorting to arbitration.

(4) For the purposes of this section the question whether an arbitration agreement is a domestic arbitration agreement shall be determined by reference to the facts at the time the legal proceedings are commenced.

Effectiveness of agreement to exclude court's jurisdiction.

87.—(1) In the case of a domestic arbitration agreement any agreement to exclude the jurisdiction of the court under—

(a) section 45 (determination of preliminary point of law), or

(b) section 69 (challenging the award: appeal on point of law),

is not effective unless entered into after the commencement of the arbitral proceedings in which the question arises or the award is made.

(2) For this purpose the commencement of the arbitral proceedings has the same meaning as in Part I (see section 14).

(3) For the purposes of this section the question whether an arbitration agreement is a domestic arbitration agreement shall be determined by reference to the facts at the time the agreement is entered into.

Power to repeal or amend sections 85 to 87.

88.—(1) The Secretary of State may by order repeal or amend the provisions of sections 85 to 87.

(2) An order under this section may contain such supplementary, incidental and transitional provisions as appear to the Secretary of State to be appropriate.

(3) An order under this section shall be made by statutory instrument and no such order shall be made unless a draft of it has been laid before and approved by a resolution of each House of Parliament.

Consumer arbitration agreements

89.—(1) The following sections extend the application of the Unfair Terms in Consumer Contracts Regulations 1994 in relation to a term which constitutes an arbitration agreement.

For this purpose "arbitration agreement" means an agreement to submit to arbitration present or future disputes or differences (whether or not contractual).

(2) In those sections "the Regulations" means those regulations and includes any regulations amending or replacing those regulations.

(3) Those sections apply whatever the law applicable to the arbitration agreement.

Application of unfair terms regulations to consumer arbitration agreements.
S.I. 1994/3159

90. The Regulations apply where the consumer is a legal person as they apply where the consumer is a natural person.

Regulations apply where consumer is a legal person.

91.—(1) A term which constitutes an arbitration agreement is unfair for the purposes of the Regulations so far as it relates to a claim for a pecuniary remedy which does not exceed the amount specified by order for the purposes of this section.

(2) Orders under this section may make different provision for different cases and for different purposes.

(3) The power to make orders under this section is exercisable—

(a) for England and Wales, by the Secretary of State with the concurrence of the Lord Chancellor,

(b) for Scotland, by the Secretary of State with the concurrence of the Lord Advocate, and

(c) for Northern Ireland, by the Department of Economic Development for Northern Ireland with the concurrence of the Lord Chancellor.

(4) Any such order for England and Wales or Scotland shall be made by statutory instrument which shall be subject to annulment in pursuance of a resolution of either House of Parliament.

(5) Any such order for Northern Ireland shall be a statutory rule for the purposes of the Statutory Rules (Northern Ireland) Order 1979 and shall be subject to negative resolution, within the meaning of section 41(6) of the Interpretation Act (Northern Ireland) 1954.

Arbitration agreement unfair where modest amount sought.

S.I. 1979/1573 (N.I. 12).
1954 c. 33 (N.I.).

Small claims arbitration in the county court

92. Nothing in Part I of this Act applies to arbitration under section 64 of the County Courts Act 1984.

Exclusion of Part I in relation to small claims arbitration in the county court.
1984 c. 28.

Appointment of judges as arbitrators

Appointment of
judges as
arbitrators.

93.—(1) A judge of the Commercial Court or an official referee may, if in all the circumstances he thinks fit, accept appointment as a sole arbitrator or as umpire by or by virtue of an arbitration agreement.

(2) A judge of the Commercial Court shall not do so unless the Lord Chief Justice has informed him that, having regard to the state of business in the High Court and the Crown Court, he can be made available.

(3) An official referee shall not do so unless the Lord Chief Justice has informed him that, having regard to the state of official referees' business, he can be made available.

(4) The fees payable for the services of a judge of the Commercial Court or official referee as arbitrator or umpire shall be taken in the High Court.

(5) In this section—

"arbitration agreement" has the same meaning as in Part I; and

1981 c. 54.

"official referee" means a person nominated under section 68(1)(a) of the Supreme Court Act 1981 to deal with official referees' business.

(6) The provisions of Part I of this Act apply to arbitration before a person appointed under this section with the modifications specified in Schedule 2.

Statutory arbitrations

Application of
Part I to statutory
arbitrations.

94.—(1) The provisions of Part I apply to every arbitration under an enactment (a "statutory arbitration"), whether the enactment was passed or made before or after the commencement of this Act, subject to the adaptations and exclusions specified in sections 95 to 98.

(2) The provisions of Part I do not apply to a statutory arbitration if or to the extent that their application—

(a) is inconsistent with the provisions of the enactment concerned, with any rules or procedure authorised or recognised by it, or

(b) is excluded by any other enactment.

(3) In this section and the following provisions of this Part "enactment"—

1978 c. 30.

(a) in England and Wales, includes an enactment contained in subordinate legislation within the meaning of the Interpretation Act 1978;

1954 c. 33 (N.I.).

(b) in Northern Ireland, means a statutory provision within the meaning of section 1(f) of the Interpretation Act (Northern Ireland) 1954.

General
adaptation of
provisions in
relation to
statutory
arbitrations.

95.—(1) The provisions of Part I apply to a statutory arbitration—

(a) as if the arbitration were pursuant to an arbitration agreement and as if the enactment were that agreement, and

(b) as if the persons by and against whom a claim subject to arbitration in pursuance of the enactment may be or has been made were parties to that agreement.

(2) Every statutory arbitration shall be taken to have its seat in England and Wales or, as the case may be, in Northern Ireland.

96.—(1) The following provisions of Part I apply to a statutory arbitration with the following adaptations.

(2) In section 30(1) (competence of tribunal to rule on its own jurisdiction), the reference in paragraph (a) to whether there is a valid arbitration agreement shall be construed as a reference to whether the enactment applies to the dispute or difference in question.

(3) Section 35 (consolidation of proceedings and concurrent hearings) applies only so as to authorise the consolidation of proceedings, or concurrent hearings in proceedings, under the same enactment.

(4) Section 46 (rules applicable to substance of dispute) applies with the omission of subsection (1)(b) (determination in accordance with considerations agreed by parties).

Specific adaptations of provisions in relation to statutory arbitrations.

97. The following provisions of Part I do not apply in relation to a statutory arbitration—

(a) section 8 (whether agreement discharged by death of a party);

(b) section 12 (power of court to extend agreed time limits);

(c) sections 9(5), 10(2) and 71(4) (restrictions on effect of provision that award condition precedent to right to bring legal proceedings).

Provisions excluded from applying to statutory arbitrations.

98.—(1) The Secretary of State may make provision by regulations for adapting or excluding any provision of Part I in relation to statutory arbitrations in general or statutory arbitrations of any particular description.

(2) The power is exercisable whether the enactment concerned is passed or made before or after the commencement of this Act.

(3) Regulations under this section shall be made by statutory instrument which shall be subject to annulment in pursuance of a resolution of either House of Parliament.

Power to make further provision by regulations.

PART III

RECOGNITION AND ENFORCEMENT OF CERTAIN FOREIGN AWARDS

Enforcement of Geneva Convention awards

99. Part II of the Arbitration Act 1950 (enforcement of certain foreign awards) continues to apply in relation to foreign awards within the meaning of that Part which are not also New York Convention awards.

Continuation of Part II of the Arbitration Act 1950.

1950 c. 27.

Recognition and enforcement of New York Convention awards

100.—(1) In this Part a "New York Convention award" means an award made, in pursuance of an arbitration agreement, in the territory of a state (other than the United Kingdom) which is a party to the New York Convention.

(2) For the purposes of subsection (1) and of the provisions of this Part relating to such awards—

New York Convention awards.

(a) "arbitration agreement" means an arbitration agreement in writing, and

(b) an award shall be treated as made at the seat of the arbitration, regardless of where it was signed, despatched or delivered to any of the parties.

In this subsection "agreement in writing" and "seat of the arbitration" have the same meaning as in Part I.

(3) If Her Majesty by Order in Council declares that a state specified in the Order is a party to the New York Convention, or is a party in respect of any territory so specified, the Order shall, while in force, be conclusive evidence of that fact.

(4) In this section "the New York Convention" means the Convention on the Recognition and Enforcement of Foreign Arbitral Awards adopted by the United Nations Conference on International Commercial Arbitration on 10th June 1958.

Recognition and enforcement of awards.

101.—(1) A New York Convention award shall be recognised as binding on the persons as between whom it was made, and may accordingly be relied on by those persons by way of defence, set-off or otherwise in any legal proceedings in England and Wales or Northern Ireland.

(2) A New York Convention award may, by leave of the court, be enforced in the same manner as a judgment or order of the court to the same effect.

As to the meaning of "the court" see section 105.

(3) Where leave is so given, judgment may be entered in terms of the award.

Evidence to be produced by party seeking recognition or enforcement.

102.—(1) A party seeking the recognition or enforcement of a New York Convention award must produce—

(a) the duly authenticated original award or a duly certified copy of it, and

(b) the original arbitration agreement or a duly certified copy of it.

(2) If the award or agreement is in a foreign language, the party must also produce a translation of it certified by an official or sworn translator or by a diplomatic or consular agent.

Refusal of recognition or enforcement.

103.—(1) Recognition or enforcement of a New York Convention award shall not be refused except in the following cases.

(2) Recognition or enforcement of the award may be refused if the person against whom it is invoked proves—

(a) that a party to the arbitration agreement was (under the law applicable to him) under some incapacity;

(b) that the arbitration agreement was not valid under the law to which the parties subjected it or, failing any indication thereon, under the law of the country where the award was made;

(c) that he was not given proper notice of the appointment of the arbitrator or of the arbitration proceedings or was otherwise unable to present his case;

    (d) that the award deals with a difference not contemplated by or not falling within the terms of the submission to arbitration or contains decisions on matters beyond the scope of the submission to arbitration (but see subsection (4));

    (e) that the composition of the arbitral tribunal or the arbitral procedure was not in accordance with the agreement of the parties or, failing such agreement, with the law of the country in which the arbitration took place;

    (f) that the award has not yet become binding on the parties, or has been set aside or suspended by a competent authority of the country in which, or under the law of which, it was made.

    (3) Recognition or enforcement of the award may also be refused if the award is in respect of a matter which is not capable of settlement by arbitration, or if it would be contrary to public policy to recognise or enforce the award.

    (4) An award which contains decisions on matters not submitted to arbitration may be recognised or enforced to the extent that it contains decisions on matters submitted to arbitration which can be separated from those on matters not so submitted.

    (5) Where an application for the setting aside or suspension of the award has been made to such a competent authority as is mentioned in subsection (2)(f), the court before which the award is sought to be relied upon may, if it considers it proper, adjourn the decision on the recognition or enforcement of the award.

    It may also on the application of the party claiming recognition or enforcement of the award order the other party to give suitable security.

104. Nothing in the preceding provisions of this Part affects any right to rely upon or enforce a New York Convention award at common law or under section 66.

Saving for other bases of recognition or enforcement.

PART IV

GENERAL PROVISIONS

105.—(1) In this Act "the court" means the High Court or a county court, subject to the following provisions.

    (2) The Lord Chancellor may by order make provision—

    (a) allocating proceedings under this Act to the High Court or to county courts; or

    (b) specifying proceedings under this Act which may be commenced or taken only in the High Court or in a county court.

    (3) The Lord Chancellor may by order make provision requiring proceedings of any specified description under this Act in relation to which a county court has jurisdiction to be commenced or taken in one or more specified county courts.

    Any jurisdiction so exercisable by a specified county court is exercisable throughout England and Wales or, as the case may be, Northern Ireland.

    (4) An order under this section—

    (a) may differentiate between categories of proceedings by reference to such criteria as the Lord Chancellor sees fit to specify, and

Meaning of "the court": jurisdiction of High Court and county court.

(b) may make such incidental or transitional provision as the Lord Chancellor considers necessary or expedient.

(5) An order under this section for England and Wales shall be made by statutory instrument which shall be subject to annulment in pursuance of a resolution of either House of Parliament.

S.I. 1979/1573 (N.I. 12).

1946 c. 36.

(6) An order under this section for Northern Ireland shall be a statutory rule for the purposes of the Statutory Rules (Northern Ireland) Order 1979 which shall be subject to annulment in pursuance of a resolution of either House of Parliament in like manner as a statutory instrument and section 5 of the Statutory Instruments Act 1946 shall apply accordingly.

Crown application.

106.—(1) Part I of this Act applies to any arbitration agreement to which Her Majesty, either in right of the Crown or of the Duchy of Lancaster or otherwise, or the Duke of Cornwall, is a party.

(2) Where Her Majesty is party to an arbitration agreement otherwise than in right of the Crown, Her Majesty shall be represented for the purposes of any arbitral proceedings—

(a) where the agreement was entered into by Her Majesty in right of the Duchy of Lancaster, by the Chancellor of the Duchy or such person as he may appoint, and

(b) in any other case, by such person as Her Majesty may appoint in writing under the Royal Sign Manual.

(3) Where the Duke of Cornwall is party to an arbitration agreement, he shall be represented for the purposes of any arbitral proceedings by such person as he may appoint.

(4) References in Part I to a party or the parties to the arbitration agreement or to arbitral proceedings shall be construed, where subsection (2) or (3) applies, as references to the person representing Her Majesty or the Duke of Cornwall.

Consequential amendments and repeals.

107.—(1) The enactments specified in Schedule 3 are amended in accordance with that Schedule, the amendments being consequential on the provisions of this Act.

(2) The enactments specified in Schedule 4 are repealed to the extent specified.

Extent.

108.—(1) The provisions of this Act extend to England and Wales and, except as mentioned below, to Northern Ireland.

(2) The following provisions of Part II do not extend to Northern Ireland—

section 92 (exclusion of Part I in relation to small claims arbitration in the county court), and

section 93 and Schedule 2 (appointment of judges as arbitrators).

(3) Sections 89, 90 and 91 (consumer arbitration agreements) extend to Scotland and the provisions of Schedules 3 and 4 (consequential amendments and repeals) extend to Scotland so far as they relate to enactments which so extend, subject as follows.

(4) The repeal of the Arbitration Act 1975 extends only to England and   1975 c. 3.
Wales and Northern Ireland.

109.—(1) The provisions of this Act come into force on such day as the   Commencement.
Secretary of State may appoint by order made by statutory instrument,
and different days may be appointed for different purposes.

(2) An order under subsection (1) may contain such transitional
provisions as appear to the Secretary of State to be appropriate.

110. This Act may be cited as the Arbitration Act 1996.   Short title.

Case Notes

Aughton Ltd v M F Kent Services Ltd
[1991] 57 BLR 1

In a sub-subcontract between the plaintiff and the defendants formed partly orally and partly in writing, the question arose as to whether an arbitration agreement had been incorporated by reference. It was decided that the parties had agreed at a meeting to incorporate the whole of the subcontract conditions, and that it was possible to modify the appropriate arbitration clauses so that they applied to the parties' contract. However, the incorporation by reference failed, as the parties had not specifically referred to the arbitration clauses, only to the subcontract as a whole.

Cape Durasteel Ltd v Rosser and Russell Building Services Ltd
[1995] 46 Con LR 75

The defendants were subcontractors and the plaintiffs sub-subcontractors in a contract to refurbish the East Market Building at Smithfield. The contract between the defendants and the main contractor incorporated the terms of the JCT Works Contract Conditions (Works Contract/2). The sub-subcontract was on the defendants' standard subcontract order terms and conditions. The plaintiff began an action against the defendant to recover the unpaid balance of the price. The claim was disputed by the defendant, who sought a stay on the action on the grounds that there was a binding arbitration agreement between the parties. Clause 23 of the defendants' standard terms provided:

'23   Settlement of Disputes
23.1   In the event of any dispute arising out of or in connection with the Sub-Contract the parties agree to refer such dispute to adjudication to a person agreed upon or upon failing agreement to some person appointed by the President for the time being of the Chartered Institute of Building Services Engineers.'

It was held that the use of the word 'adjudication' is not in itself decisive as to whether the agreement between the parties constituted an agreement to arbitrate; this was a question of whether the agreement did in the particular circumstances have the essential features of arbitration. Clause 23.1 was held to constitute such an agreement. As this was the only method of dispute resolution provided for, and there was no possibility of review, to interpret it as a reference to an expert would affect the rights of the parties.

Cruden Construction Ltd v Commission for the New Towns
[1994] 75 BLR 134

Cruden built 145 dwellings for the Commission, who then sold them to a housing association. The housing association later issued a writ against the Commission regarding defects in the dwellings. The Commission's solicitors wrote to Cruden's solicitors referring to the writ and asking whether they had authority to receive a notice to arbitrate under the main contract. Cruden's solicitors replied stating that while they did not admit the truth of any matters in the claim, they did have authority to receive a notice. This exchange did not constitute a 'dispute' under the JCT 63 arbitration clause, as no specific claim had been made against Cruden.

Higgs & Hill Building Ltd v Campbell Denis Ltd and Another
[1982] 28 BLR 47

The plaintiffs were main contractors and the defendants nominated subcontractors, with a subcontract on the NFBTE/FASS 'green' form, with a clause which stated:

'Provided that if the dispute or difference between the Contractor and the Sub-contractor is substantially the same as a matter which is in dispute or difference between the Contractor and Employer under the main contract the Contractor and Sub-contractor hereby agree that such dispute or difference shall be referred to an arbitrator appointed or to be appointed pursuant to the terms of the main contract ...'

The defendants issued a notice to arbitrate and an arbitrator was appointed by the RICS. The main contractors challenged the arbitrator's jurisdiction at the preliminary meeting and at the hearing, as they wished to refer the dispute to an arbitrator to be appointed under the main contract. It was held that the appointment of the subcontract arbitrator could not be revoked, and that he had jurisdiction to decide the disputes referred to him.

Hyundai Engineering and Construction Co Ltd v Active Building and Civil Construction PteE Ltd
[1988] 45 BLR 52

The plaintiffs were main contractors and the defendants one of their subcontractors, on a subcontract with an arbitration clause similar to that on the NFBTE/FASS 'green' form which stated:

'Provided that if the dispute or difference between the Contractor and the Sub-contractor is substantially the same as a matter which is in dispute or difference between the Contractor and Employer under the main contract the Contractor and Sub-contractor hereby agree that such dispute or difference shall be referred to an arbitrator appointed or to be appointed pursuant to the terms of the main contract ...'

The defendants referred to arbitration disputes concerning measurement, variations etc. It was common ground that some of the disputes were substantially the same as matters already referred to an arbitrator under the main contract. The plaintiffs sought a declaration that all disputes should be referred to the main contract arbitration. It was held that there were a number of separate disputes, and that only those which were substantially the same must be referred to the main contract arbitration. The word 'dispute' meant a dispute on a specific item or at least those grouped under a specific heading. The clause did not give the subcontract arbitrator the right to determine his own jurisdiction – the question of which disputes concern matters substantially the same would need to be determined by a court.

M J Gleeson Group plc v Wyatt of Snetterton Ltd
[1994] 72 BLR 15

Gleeson were main contractors and Wyatt subcontractors under the FCEC standard form of subcontract for use with the ICE standard form of contract. The subcontract contained the clause:

'If any dispute arises in connection with the Main Contract and the Contractor is of the opinion that such dispute touches or concerns the Sub-Contract work, then provided an arbitrator has not already been agreed or appointed in pursuance of the preceding sub-clause the Contractor may by notice in writing to the subcontractor require that any such dispute ... shall be dealt with jointly with the dispute under the Main Contract.'

After receiving the subcontractors' final account, the engineer identified areas of dispute between the main contractor and the employer relating to the account. The subcontractors requested the President of the ICE to appoint an arbitrator, but the appointment was not made for another eight months. In the meantime the main contractor had given notice in writing requesting the disputes to be dealt with jointly. Once the arbitrator was appointed the Main Contractor issued proceedings in the High Court, and the Official Referee at first instance held that the arbitrator did not have jurisdiction. The declaration was upheld on appeal. (Note the difference in the above wording to NSC/C. The above proviso could be invoked as soon as a dispute has arisen under the main contract, whereas with the JCT wording an arbitrator must have been appointed – *see Trafalgar House v Railtrack* below.)

Metro-Cammell Hong Kong Ltd v FKI Engineering plc
[1996] 77 BLR 84

FKI supplied alternators to MC which were faulty. FKI undertook repair work and MC paid them £100,000 on account which they stated to be 'without prejudice'. FKI then brought a claim for an additional £234,457 for repair work. MC counterclaimed for £627,000 to make the alternators fit for purpose, plus £12,640 liquidated damages. The arbitrator found that FKI were not liable for the faults and that the costs they had incurred for repair work were £95,602. Taking into account the £100,000 already paid by

MC, he ordered that FKI repay £4,457 to MC. He awarded MC £7,350 for cost of repairs they had had carried out by others. He then awarded costs on a complex basis whereby FKI were to pay MC one-third of their costs, two-thirds costs of the reference, 50% of all arbitrator's fees remaining plus one-third to MC of all arbitrator's fees paid. In doing this the arbitrator laid emphasis on the fact that FKI had not been responsible for the defects in the alternators ('this was not a dispute regarding money'), and the wide discretion available to the arbitrator in the exercise of his power to award costs.

The Official Referee found that there was no lawful basis on which such an award as to costs could have been made. The £100,000 already paid was not something that should have been taken into account. FKI had totally failed in their claim for an additional amount. The normal rule was that costs should follow the event and any discretion exercised in the departure from that should be exercised judicially. MC should have all the costs in the claim, and MC theirs in the counterclaim.

Monmouthshire County Council v Costelloe & Kemple
[1965] 5 BLR 83

During the course of a contract to carry out improvement works to the A48, a site meeting was held at which at which the defendants, who were the main contractors, indicated that they intended to make a claim for extra costs. They then wrote to the engineer stating:

'We are forced to present a claim for heavy increased costs that have been incurred through dealing with such a large volume of rock that was in no way foreseen. Prior to presenting our claims you may prefer that we have a discussion on the matter and your observations would be appreciated.'

The engineer replied refusing, with reasons, to deal with the claim. It was another two years before the contractors wrote enclosing their 'semi-final' account, where they included details of the claim regarding the rock, which the engineer rejected. The court held that a dispute had not arisen until the date of the engineer's letter rejecting the claim.

Northern Regional Health Authority v Derek Crouch Construction Company
[1984] 26 BLR 1

NRHA brought an appeal against a decision of an Official Referee to allow a stay of court proceedings where an arbitration clause existed in the contract out of which the action arose. The appeal was dismissed. The arbitration agreement was of a common format which expressly gave the arbitrator the power to 'open up, review and revise' the certificates and decisions of the architect. In considering the appeal the court considered the question of whether or not the court had a similar power. In spite of the fact that the Official Referees had been customarily opening up and reviewing certificates in the course of their judgments, and even though the precedents were few and ambiguous, the court held that the court had no such power. 'In principle, in an action based on contract the court can only enforce the agreement between the parties: it has no power to modify the agreement in any way ... In this contract the parties have agreed that certain rights and obligations are to be determined by the certificate or opinion of the architect ... In no circumstances would the court have the power to revise such certificate or opinion solely on the ground that the court would have reached a different conclusion.' (Browne-Wilkinson LJ at p29) Though the views expressed were strictly obiter, the court laid great emphasis on them and the case has been followed.

Tarmac Construction Limited v Esso Petroleum Limited
[1996] 51 CLR 187

The parties had removed the arbitration clause from a 5th edition of the ICE standard form of contract and had inserted an amended clause 66 which stated:

'If any dispute or difference of any kind shall arise between the Employer and the Engineer ... including any dispute as to any decision opinion instruction direction certificate or valuation of the Engineer ... it shall be referred to and settled by the Engineer.'

The engineer's decision was to be final and binding on the parties unless either of the parties, within a given time limit, 'require that the matter be determined by litigation'. As the matter could clearly include a dispute regarding a decision reached by the engineer, the particular wording gave the court the right to open up and review those decisions.

Trafalgar House Construction (Regions) Ltd v Railtrack plc
[1995] 75 BLR 55

Railtrack entered into a contract with Trafalgar House for reconstruction works at East Croydon Railway Station. Tarmac and Blight and White Ltd were nominated subcontractors. The main contract was JCT 80 and the subcontracts were on NSC/4. Disputes arose over extensions of time and loss and expense claims, and Tarmac and Blight and White both served notices to arbitrate, which were ineffective due to technical errors. Trafalgar House then served a notice to arbitrate on Railtrack, repeating the claims of Tarmac and Blight and White, and an arbitrator was appointed. Tarmac and Blight and White then served a valid notice on Trafalgar House who invoked the proviso of clause 38.2.1 to each nominated sub-contractor. All four parties attended a preliminary meeting, reserving their positions with respect to jurisdiction. The arbitrator then issued three Orders in each of the three arbitrations and an Order for Directions which treated the arbitration as a quadripartite arbitration, and set one hearing date for all of the matters in dispute between the parties. Trafalgar House and Railtrack applied for a declaration as to whether the arbitration was solely between them or a quadripartite arbitration, whether the Order was invalid and whether the arbitrator had misconducted the proceedings. The judge made the following findings:

- the back to back clauses effectively bound all four parties: the Employer and Contractor had accepted in advance that a third party might be enjoined in the arbitration and their further consent was not required – assuming of course that the proviso was fulfilled;
- the Employer and Contractor had accepted in advance that their dispute might be heard by an arbitrator already appointed in another arbitration;
- the back to back clauses were silent as to how the proviso was to be assessed, and by whom. It is difficult to define at an early stage in a reference whether the issues in dispute have areas in common;
- the back to back clauses could be invoked only after the first arbitrator had been appointed but before the second was appointed. Parties could reserve their positions and see how the dispute developed, but could not join the disputes once an award was 'in the offing';
- the fact that the clauses effectively brought the disputes before the same arbitrator did not set out how this was to happen. The arbitrator had to address the question as to whether there remained three separate arbitrations or whether he should use his powers of joinder to consolidate the proceedings. By immediately assuming he was dealing with a quadripartite arbitration the arbitrator had erred in law.

University of Reading v Miller Construction Ltd and David Sharp
[1994] 75 BLR 91

The University employed Miller for building work on its Institute of Food Research Laboratory under two separate contracts, one following directly after the other. The first contract did not contain an arbitration agreement whereas the second, a JCT 80 standard form, did. Clause 25 of the JCT 80 contract was amended so that a delay to the first contract would give an extension of time to the second. Following practical completion Miller issued a notice to arbitrate, claiming £1.8 million from the University. The University replied, making it clear that because of the involvement of several other parties the Official Referees' Court would be a more appropriate forum, offering to consent to the court assuming the like powers of an arbitrator. It then issued a writ against Miller, the consulting engineers and the architects.

Mr Sharp was then appointed as arbitrator following an application by Miller to the RIBA under the terms of the JCT contract. Miller also applied for a stay of the court proceedings, which was dismissed, following which Miller appealed. The University drew the dismissal of the stay to the arbitrator's attention, but he decided to continue with the reference, so the University applied for an injunction to restrain the arbitrator or Miller from proceeding.

The judge granted the injunction. The power to restrain an arbitration where court proceedings were running in parallel would be exercised where no injustice would be caused to the claimant and continuance of the arbitration would be 'oppressive, vexatious or an abuse of the process'. No injustice would be caused, as the court could determine all the issues that had been raised by the University, the University would be seriously prejudiced by a race, and the issues could only be satisfactorily resolved by involving the third parties. Even if the court were not given the arbitrator's powers to open up and review, 'the distinction between the jurisdiction of the court and that of the arbitrator is quite limited,' and the issue of quantum of direct loss and/or expense, for example, is not a matter of opinion. None of the issues about which the University sought a declaration fell within the sole province of an arbitrator.

Vascroft (Contractors) Ltd v Seeboard plc
[1996] 78 BLR 132

Vascroft (main contractors) entered into a contract with Seeboard (subcontractors) for electrical works on a form of contract based on DOM/2. Clause 38.7 stated:

'The parties hereby agree and consent pursuant to sections 1(3)(a) and 2(1)(b) of the Arbitration Act 1979 that either party
38.7.1 may appeal to the High Court on any question of law arising out of an award made in an arbitration made under this Arbitration Agreement; and
38.7.2 may apply to the High Court to determine any question of law arising in the course of the reference.'

Disputes arose on the subcontract and an arbitration was commenced. The arbitrator made an interim award on certain preliminary questions. Vascroft wished to appeal on a point of law and the question arose as to whether leave to appeal was required. The judge decided that clause 38.7 amounted to a valid consent within the meaning of S.1(3)(a) of the Arbitration Act 1979 and that leave to appeal was not required.

Index